The

Apache

THE HISTORY & CULTURE
of NATIVE AMERICANS

THE HISTORY & CULTURE of NATIVE AMERICANS

The
Apache

JOSEPH C. JASTRZEMBSKI

Series Editor
PAUL C. ROSIER

CHELSEA HOUSE
An Infobase Learning Company

Chelsea House
An imprint of Infobase Learning
132 West 31st Street
New York NY 10001

Library of Congress Cataloging-in-Publication Data
Jastrzembski, Joseph C.
     The Apache / Joseph C. Jastrzembski.
         p. cm. — (The history and culture of Native Americans)
Includes bibliographical references and index.
ISBN 978-1-60413-793-4 (hardcover)
     1. Apache Indians—History—Juvenile literature. 2. Apache Indians—Social life and customs—Juvenile literature. I. Title. II. Series.
     E99.A6J368 2011
     979.004'9725—dc22   2010052883

Chelsea House books are available at special discounts when purchased in bulk quantities for businesses, associations, institutions, or sales promotions. Please call our Special Sales Department in New York at (212) 967-8800 or (800) 322-8755.

You can find Chelsea House on the World Wide Web at
http://www.infobaselearning.com

Text design by Lina Farinella
Cover design by Alicia Post
Composition by Julie Adams
Cover printed by Yurchak Printing, Landisville, Pa.
Book printed and bound by Yurchak Printing, Landisville, Pa.
Date printed: June 2011
Printed in the United States of America

10 9 8 7 6 5 4 3 2 1

This book is printed on acid-free paper.
All links and Web addresses were checked and verified to be correct at the time of publication. Because of the dynamic nature of the Web, some addresses and links may have changed since publication and may no longer be valid.

Contents

Foreword
by Paul C. Rosier

Native American words, phrases, and tribal names are embedded in the very geography of the United States—in the names of creeks, rivers, lakes, cities, and states, including Alabama, Connecticut, Iowa, Kansas, Illinois, Missouri, Oklahoma, and many others. Yet Native Americans remain the most misunderstood ethnic group in the United States. This is a result of limited coverage of Native American history in middle schools, high schools, and colleges; poor coverage of contemporary Native American issues in the news media; and stereotypes created by Hollywood movies, sporting events, and TV shows.

Two newspaper articles about American Indians caught my eye in recent months. Paired together, they provide us with a good introduction to the experiences of American Indians today: first, how they are stereotyped and turned into commodities; and second, how they see themselves being a part of the United States and of the wider world. (Note: I use the terms *Native Americans* and *American Indians* interchangeably; both terms are considered appropriate.)

In the first article, "Humorous Souvenirs to Some, Offensive Stereotypes to Others," written by Carol Berry in *Indian Country Today,* I read that tourist shops in Colorado were selling "souvenir" T-shirts portraying American Indians as drunks. "My Indian name is Runs with Beer," read one T-shirt offered in Denver. According to the article, the T-shirts are "the kind of stereotype-reinforcing products also seen in nearby Boulder, Estes Park, and likely other Colorado communities, whether as part of the tourism trade or as everyday merchandise." No other ethnic group in the United States is stereotyped in such a public fashion. In addition, Native people are used to sell a range of consumer goods, including the Jeep Cherokee, Red Man chewing tobacco, Land O'Lakes butter, and other items that either objectify or insult them, such as cigar store Indians. As importantly, non-Indians learn about American Indian history and culture through sports teams such as the Atlanta Braves, Cleveland Indians, Florida State Seminoles, or Washington Redskins, whose name many American Indians consider a racist insult; dictionaries define *redskin* as a "disparaging" or "offensive" term for American Indians. When fans in Atlanta do their "tomahawk chant" at Braves baseball games, they perform two inappropriate and related acts: One, they perpetuate a stereotype of American Indians as violent; and two, they tell a historical narrative that covers up the violent ways that Georgians treated the Cherokee during the Removal period of the 1830s.

The second article, written by Melissa Pinion-Whitt of the San Bernardino *Sun* addressed an important but unknown dimension of Native American societies that runs counter to the irresponsible and violent image created by products and sporting events. The article, "San Manuels Donate $1.7 M for Aid to Haiti," described a Native American community that had sent aid to Haiti after it was devastated in January 2010 by an earthquake that killed more than 200,000 people, injured hundreds of thousands more, and destroyed the Haitian capital. The San Manuel Band of Mission Indians in California donated $1.7 million to help relief efforts in Haiti; San Manuel children held fund-raisers to collect additional donations. For the San Manuel Indians it was nothing new; in 2007 they had donated $1 million to help Sudanese refugees in Darfur. San Manuel also contributed $700,000 to relief efforts following Hurricane Katrina and Hurricane Rita, and donated $1 million in 2007 for wildfire recovery in Southern California.

Such generosity is consistent with many American Indian nations' cultural practices, such as the "give-away," in which wealthy tribal members give to the needy, and the "potlatch," a winter gift-giving ceremony and feast tradition shared by tribes in the Pacific

Northwest. And it is consistent with historical accounts of American Indians' generosity. For example, in 1847 Cherokee and Choctaw, who had recently survived their forced march on a "Trail of Tears" from their homelands in the American South to present-day Oklahoma, sent aid to Irish families after reading of the potato famine, which created a similar forced migration of Irish. A Cherokee newspaper editorial, quoted in Christine Kinealy's *The Great Irish Famine: Impact, Ideology, and Rebellion,* explained that the Cherokee "will be richly repaid by the consciousness of having done a good act, by the moral effect it will produce abroad." During and after World War II, nine Pueblo communities in New Mexico offered to donate food to the hungry in Europe, after Pueblo army veterans told stories of suffering they had witnessed while serving in the United States armed forces overseas. Considering themselves a part of the wider world, Native people have reached beyond their borders, despite their own material poverty, to help create a peaceful world community.

American Indian nations have demonstrated such generosity within the United States, especially in recent years. After the terrorist attacks of September 11, 2001, the Lakota Sioux in South Dakota offered police officers and emergency medical personnel to New York City to help with relief efforts; Indian nations across the country sent millions of dollars to help the victims of the attacks. As an editorial in the *Native American Times* newspaper explained on September 12, 2001, "American Indians love this country like no other. . . . Today, we are all New Yorkers."

Indeed, Native Americans have sacrificed their lives in defending the United States from its enemies in order to maintain their right to be both American and Indian. As the volumes in this series tell us, Native Americans patriotically served as soldiers (including as "code talkers") during World War I and World War II, as well as during the Korean War, the Vietnam War, and, after 9/11, the wars in Afghanistan and Iraq. Native soldiers, men and women, do so today by the tens of thousands because they believe in America, an

America that celebrates different cultures and peoples. Sgt. Leonard Gouge, a Muscogee Creek, explained it best in an article in *Cherokee News Path* in discussing his post-9/11 army service. He said he was willing to serve his country abroad because "by supporting the American way of life, I am preserving the Indian way of life."

This new Chelsea House series has two main goals. The first is to document the rich diversity of American Indian societies and the ways their cultural practices and traditions have evolved over time. The second goal is to provide the reader with coverage of the complex relationships that have developed between non-Indians and Indians over the past several hundred years. This history helps to explain why American Indians consider themselves both American and Indian and why they see preserving this identity as a strength of the American way of life, as evidence to the rest of the world that America is a champion of cultural diversity and religious freedom. By exploring Native Americans' cultural diversity and their contributions to the making of the United States, these volumes confront the stereotypes that paint all American Indians as the same and portray them as violent; as "drunks," as those Colorado T-shirts do; or as rich casino owners, as many news accounts do.

* * *

Each of the 14 volumes in this series is written by a scholar who shares my conviction that young adult readers are both fascinated by Native American history and culture and have not been provided with sufficient material to properly understand the diverse nature of this complex history and culture. The authors themselves represent a varied group that includes university teachers and professional writers, men and women, and Native and non-Native. To tell these fascinating stories, this talented group of scholars has examined an incredible variety of sources, both the primary sources that historical actors have created and the secondary sources that historians and anthropologists have written to make sense of the past.

Although the 14 Indian nations (also called tribes and communities) selected for this series have different histories and cultures, they all share certain common experiences. In particular, they had to face an American empire that spread westward in the eighteenth and nineteenth centuries, causing great trauma and change for all Native people in the process. Because each volume documents American Indians' experiences dealing with powerful non-Indian institutions and ideas, I outline below the major periods and features of federal Indian policymaking in order to provide a frame of reference for complex processes of change with which American Indians had to contend. These periods—Assimilation, Indian New Deal, Termination, Red Power, and Self-determination—and specific acts of legislation that define them—in particular the General Allotment Act, the Indian Reorganization Act, and the Indian Self-determination and Education Assistance Act—will appear in all the volumes, especially in the latter chapters.

In 1851, the commissioner of the federal Bureau of Indian Affairs (BIA) outlined a three-part program for subduing American Indians militarily and assimilating them into the United States: concentration, domestication, and incorporation. In the first phase, the federal government waged war with the American Indian nations of the American West in order to "concentrate" them on reservations, away from expanding settlements of white Americans and immigrants. Some American Indian nations experienced terrible violence in resisting federal troops and state militia; others submitted peacefully and accepted life on a reservation. During this phase, roughly from the 1850s to the 1880s, the U.S. government signed hundreds of treaties with defeated American Indian nations. These treaties "reserved" to these American Indian nations specific territory as well as the use of natural resources. And they provided funding for the next phase of "domestication."

During the domestication phase, roughly the 1870s to the early 1900s, federal officials sought to remake American Indians in the mold of white Americans. Through the Civilization Program, which actually started with President Thomas Jefferson, federal officials sent religious missionaries, farm instructors, and teachers to the newly created reservations in an effort to "kill the Indian to save the man," to use a phrase of that time. The ultimate goal was to extinguish American Indian cultural traditions and turn American Indians into Christian yeoman farmers. The most important piece of legislation in this period was the General Allotment Act (or Dawes Act), which mandated that American Indian nations sell much of their territory to white farmers and use the proceeds to farm on what was left of their homelands. The program was a failure, for the most part, because white farmers got much of the best arable land in the process. Another important part of the domestication agenda was the federal boarding school program, which required all American Indian children to attend schools to further their rejection of Indian ways and the adoption of non-Indian ways. The goal of federal reformers, in sum, was to incorporate (or assimilate) American Indians into American society as individual citizens and not as groups with special traditions and religious practices.

During the 1930s some federal officials came to believe that American Indians deserved the right to practice their own religion and sustain their identity as Indians, arguing that such diversity made America stronger. During the Indian New Deal period of the 1930s, BIA commissioner John Collier devised the Indian Reorganization Act (IRA), which passed in 1934, to give American Indian nations more power, not less. Not all American Indians supported the IRA, but most did. They were eager to improve their reservations, which suffered from tremendous poverty that resulted in large measure from federal policies such as the General Allotment Act.

Some federal officials opposed the IRA, however, and pushed for the assimilation of American Indians in a movement called Termination. The two main goals of Termination advocates, during the 1950s and 1960s, were to end (terminate) the federal reservation system and American Indians' political sovereignty derived from treaties and to relocate American Indians from rural reservations to urban areas. These coercive federal assimilation policies in turn generated resistance from Native Americans, including young activists who helped to create the so-called Red Power era of the 1960s and 1970s, which coincided with the African-American civil rights movement. This resistance led to the federal government's rejection of Termination policies in 1970. And in 1975 the U.S. Congress passed the Indian Self-determination and Education Assistance Act, which made it the government's policy to support American Indians' right to determine the future of their communities. Congress then passed legislation to help American Indian nations to improve reservation life; these acts strengthened American Indians' religious freedom, political sovereignty, and economic opportunity.

All American Indians, especially those in the western United States, were affected in some way by the various federal policies described above. But it is important to highlight the fact that each American Indian community responded in different ways to these pressures for change, both the detribalization policies of assimilation and the retribalization policies of self-determination. There is no one group of "Indians." American Indians were and still are a very diverse group. Some embraced the assimilation programs of the federal government and rejected the old traditions; others refused to adopt non-Indian customs or did so selectively, on their own terms. Most American Indians, as I noted above, maintain a dual identity of American and Indian.

Today, there are more than 550 American Indian (and Alaska Natives) nations recognized by the federal government. They have a legal and political status similar to states, but they have special rights and privileges that are the result of congressional acts and the hundreds of treaties that still govern federal-Indian relations today. In July 2008, the total population of American Indians (and Alaska Natives) was 4.9 million, representing about 1.6 percent of the United States population. The state with the highest number of American Indians is California, followed by Oklahoma, home to the Cherokee (the largest American Indian nation in terms of population), and then Arizona, home to the Navajo (the second-largest American Indian nation). All told, roughly half of the American Indian population lives in urban areas; the other half lives on reservations and in other rural parts of the country. Like all their fellow American citizens, American Indians pay federal taxes, obey federal laws, and vote in federal, state, and local elections; they also participate in the democratic processes of their American Indian nations, electing judges, politicians, and other civic officials.

This series on the history and culture of Native Americans celebrates their diversity and differences as well as the ways they have strengthened the broader community of America. Ronnie Lupe, the chairman of the White Mountain Apache government in Arizona, once addressed questions from non-Indians as to "why Indians serve the United States with such distinction and honor?" Lupe, a Korean War veteran, answered those questions during the Gulf War of 1991–1992, in which Native American soldiers served to protect the independence of the Kuwaiti people. He explained in "Chairman's Corner" in the *Fort Apache Scout* that "our loyalty to the United States goes beyond our need to defend our home and reservation lands. . . . Only a few in this country really understand that the indigenous people are a national treasure. Our values have the potential of creating the social, environmental, and spiritual healing that could make this country truly great."

—Paul C. Rosier
Associate Professor of History
Villanova University

In the
Beginning

The woman sat by the fire playing with her baby. She helped him take his first tentative steps, guiding him by his hands as he placed one foot uncertainly in front of the other. Slowly, over many days, his balance improved and he could toddle around the camp under his mother's watchful eye. Then they would play the game in which she would hold out her arms and he would run into her embrace, swept up and hugged close, mother and son smiling and laughing in delight.

One day, however, as they played that familiar game, the mother heard a loud, crashing noise. Something large was swiftly approaching the camp, crushing the brush beneath its monstrous feet. Barely in time, she hid her son in a hole under the fire, a place of safety she had dug just for this event.

"Where is the child," the giant demanded. "I know you have a baby. I see his tracks before me. Give him to me now. You know I will let no other humans live."

"I have no child," she said. "I am all alone. But I am sad and so pretend that I have a baby to keep me company. I made those tracks myself."

"Show me how you did it," the giant roared.

And so the woman took her fist and pressed it into the earth. Then, using the tip of her finger, she added five little toe marks. A baby's footprint! The giant looked at the footprint for a long time, and finally, with a snort of disgust, it strode away.

Years later the woman sent her son out into the world, armed with a bow and arrow. For the time had come to rid the world of monsters. When the giant saw the young man, he picked up a pine log and fit it into his bow. As the mighty arrow neared the young man, he bowed his head and prayed to his father, the power of storm and lightning, and the arrow missed him. Three times more the giant launched his massive arrows, and three times more he missed. And then the young man, Child of the Water, now Killer of Enemies, shot his first arrow. The giant was unafraid. He wore four coats of stone armor. What could hurt him? But the first arrow shattered the first layer of rock. Soon the second and third layers lay broken as well, revealing the last, covering his beating heart. And so the young man readied his last arrow and let it fly. The giant crashed to the ground, four small hills crushed beneath his bulk. Later more adventures followed—the slaying of the eagles, the antelopes that killed with a glance, and the monster buffalo defeated with the help of a gopher. Eventually Child of the Water cleared the earth of monsters, and his people, the Apache, could now live and thrive. This book is their story.

THE PEOPLE

The stories of Child of the Water and his mother, White Painted Woman, reveal a great deal about the people who first told these tales, the Apache. Like White Painted Woman and Child of the Water, they drew on the strength and resilience of family; relied on their wits, cunning, and adaptability; invoked the aid of animal

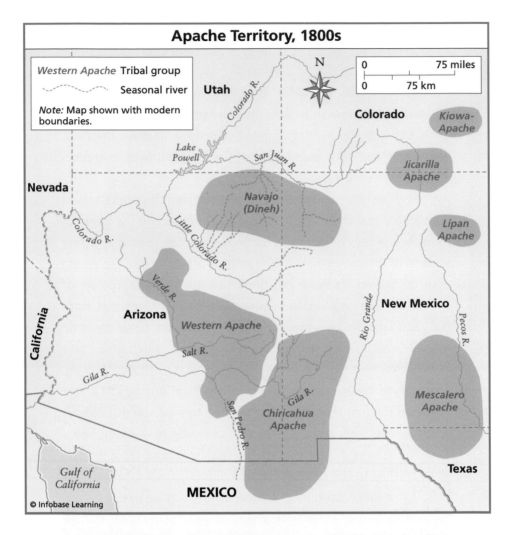

Apache Territory, 1800s

Western Apache Tribal group

⁓⁓ Seasonal river

Note: Map shown with modern boundaries.

N

0   75 miles
0   75 km

Utah

Colorado R.

Colorado

Kiowa-Apache

Nevada

Lake Powell

San Juan R.

Jicarilla Apache

Navajo (Dineh)

Lipan Apache

Colorado R.

Little Colorado R.

Verde R.

Arizona

Western Apache

New Mexico

Rio Grande

Pecos R.

Salt R.

Gila R.

San Pedro R.

Gila R.

Chiricahua Apache

Mescalero Apache

California

Gulf of California

MEXICO

Texas

© Infobase Learning

The Apache comprise several different groups of indigenous people located throughout the Southwest and the Great Plains.

helpers and other forces; and showed unflinching patience and determination in order to navigate an uncertain and dangerous world. Never as numerous as other American Indian tribes, the Apache nevertheless survived against myriad challenges. Today, Apache people are found all over the United States, but their historical territories are in the American Southwest, the southern plains, and northern Mexico. Most still live in the states of Arizona, New Mexico, and Oklahoma, where the principal Apache reservations are located. These include the Jicarilla Apache Reservation of northern New Mexico and the Mescalero Apache Reservation to the south, home not only to the Mescalero but also the descendants of the Lipan and Chiricahua Apache; the Western Apache reservations of Arizona; and the Fort Sill Apache and Plains Apache of Oklahoma. Notwithstanding these largely geographic divisions, the Apache as a whole draw on the strength and wisdom of those who came before to maintain themselves as a distinct people within American society.

Like many other American Indian groups, the Apache have a name bestowed on them from the outside. Linguists, researchers who study languages and their relationships, still debate whether the term *Apache* derives from Zuni, Yavapai, or other American Indian languages. In their own dialects, the various peoples who comprise the Apache simply call themselves "the people." Linguists have found similarities between the Apache dialects and those spoken by other groups in northern California, southern Oregon, and the interiors of Alaska and Canada, classifying these languages as part of the Athapascan family. In fact, many linguists see interior Alaska and Canada, or the western sub-Arctic, as the ancestral cradle for all Athapascan speakers, which would mean that the ancestors of the Apache must have made their way southward over many years, slowly covering the vast distances that would eventually take them into the American Southwest and the southern plains, the place they would come to see as their homeland.

Archaeology, the study of things used or constructed by ancient peoples, provides more insight into the earliest of these Apache peoples, although much speculation remains, particularly as to why the Athapascan language family members diverged over time. What seems probable is that the earliest Apache were a highly adaptable mountain people like later sub-Arctic Indian groups. In the harshness of the western sub-Arctic, mountains provided a variety of resources, from wild game to wild plant life, that could be exploited seasonally by small, highly mobile groups of people. From the mountains, the Apache could also move out to strike at other kinds of resources, caribou, for instance, traveling in immense herds. Finally, the mountains represented a network of "roads," vast ranges spreading far into the north, the northeast, and especially the southeast. Following the ranges to the south, the earliest Apache eventually connected to the Rockies and into the mountains and plains of what is now the United States.

Archaeologists construct their picture of these early Apache peoples through such things as spear points, stone knives, and other material objects, some of the most extraordinary of which are elaborate stone structures, more than 300 feet (91 meters) in length, built high above the timberline in north-central Colorado in the Front Range of the Rocky Mountains, probably around 1000 A.D. These were game-drive systems, funnel-shaped stone walls used to channel herds of game. Driven into the wide opening of the wall system by the shouts and cries of Apache, game animals such as elk or deer were increasingly concentrated as the walls narrowed, until finally their heaving, shifting mass was set upon by waiting hunters. But like the earlier hunting and gathering peoples of the sub-Arctic, these Apache also followed a seasonal sequence of movements, launching from the sheltering reaches of the Front Range in the early spring into southern Wyoming, where quartz outcroppings could be quarried to make tools. Summers then took them into the high country, and finally autumns brought them back to the Front Range and the great cooperative game drives that culminated in the butchering and smoking of prodigious amounts of meat. Finally the growing cold and the onset of winter broke up these gatherings, and small groups of Apache moved to their winter camps at the foot of the Front Range.

Historians now pick up the story, gleaned from the records left by Spanish explorers in the sixteenth century. In the 1540s, the expedition of Francisco Vásquez de Coronado almost certainly encountered the Apache while wandering the staked plains of Texas searching for elusive cities of gold. Called *Querechos* by the Spanish, these Apache traveled the plains in small groups on foot with their packs of dogs. To the Spanish, the Apache were a rude, savage people and the plains were an inhospitable landscape. To the Apache, however, the plains, like the mountains, presented a profusion of exploitable resources, among these deer and antelope, and along the few sheltered watercourses, wild berries and other plants. And of course, there were the great herds of buffalo, providing not only meat but also hides for clothing and shelter. Using cooperative hunting techniques honed over the centuries and relying on deadly accuracy with bows and arrows, the Apache took so many buffalo that their excess could be used in trade.

Although the Apache diet was rich in proteins, wild plant resources did not provide sufficient carbohydrates. South and west of the plains, however, the various Pueblo peoples of the Rio Grande Valley cultivated, in good years, surpluses of corn or maize that could be exchanged for the meat and hides of the Apache. These villages welcomed caravans of Apache, their dogs straining under loads of dried meat or hides. Haggling would go on for days, even weeks, and then the Apache would depart, loaded with corn, fresh and dried squash, and beans.

This glimpse of sixteenth-century Apache life on the plains reconstructed from Spanish records provides at best an incomplete picture of the Apache. These Apache may have hugged the eastern slopes of the Rocky Mountains, skirting the plains as they moved steadily south and east, traveling between mountains and plains as their quest for subsistence took them. Others, however, oriented themselves farther to the west, where a complicated array of mountain ranges continues west to the edge of the Great Basin and southward into Mexico. As a result, slight cultural differences developed over time between the eastern- and western-oriented Apache people.

Some of these differences affected language as the wide dispersal of the people lent itself to the development of different Apache dialects. Some of these differences grew from subsistence needs and adaptations. Other differences developed as a result of contact with non-Apache, whether one group relied solely on hunting and gathering or another experimented with agriculture, for example. None, however, lost their affinity for the mountains. Coupled with their extraordinary mobility, this allowed them to maintain a sense of connectedness, a sense of common identity as "the people."

THE CULTURE OF "THE PEOPLE"

Culture can be thought of as the different ways that different groups of human beings do things. Anthropologists and ethnographers study these differences to gain an understanding of how cultures "work," how people organize their lives. Sometimes the focus is on the different tools humans develop and use; at other times the focus is on the different institutions that people develop. Most importantly, culture involves the different beliefs that people have about themselves and the world around them. Anthropologists believe that by the time the Apache entered the Southwest, certain cultural patterns had already been established; others would develop as the Apache adapted to their new environment and circumstances.

Once in the Southwest the Apache, for the most part, continued their hunting way of life. The plains furnished buffalo, the mountains yielded deer, the lower elevations antelope. Boys could take smaller game as they learned the rudiments of hunting. Eventually cattle and horses, both introduced by the Spanish, would also provide needed protein. In the Southwest, the gathering of wild plant resources assumed greater importance, with the warmer climate furnishing more plant varieties than the sub-Arctic. As a result, women, as the primary gatherers, contributed at least an equal, if not greater, amount to subsistence than the hunting men. To some degree, gathering influenced Apache movements as different kinds of food came available seasonally. Early spring to late fall saw Apache women gathering varieties of nuts, berries, seeds, roots, and cacti in a number of different ecological zones ranging from mountains to deserts. Processing and storing food occupied much time as well. Mescal (a kind of cactus) became one of the most important dietary staples. Gathered communally by the women, it could be steamed, dried in the sun, and stored, providing a sweet, nutritious food for many months, particularly through the winter.

The contribution of women to the subsistence quest may have had implications for their status as well. A married Apache man, for instance, most often lived with his wife's family and showed particular respect to his mother-in-law. Certainly among the Apache, White Painted Woman, also called White Shell Woman, played a major role in their belief system. Moreover, ceremonies to mark the onset of female puberty were arguably the most developed of Apache rituals. During the four days of the puberty rite, Apache regarded the young women making the transition to adulthood to be the embodiment of White Painted Woman and therefore imbued with power, particularly for healing.

As a hunting and gathering people, the Apache maintained themselves in small groups, scattered over a wide area. These small groups were made up of a number of family units that cooperated together, largely to exploit resources from a given locale. Within the family unit, grandparents received particular attention as their wisdom and knowledge provided guidance to all and insight into proper behavior for the young. Yet within each group as a whole, headmen usually emerged, valued for their leadership skills. Key to leadership was persuasion. Apache leaders had to convince their followers that a given course of action was beneficial. If dissatisfied with the results, an Apache family could choose at any time to strike out on its own or join another group. The Spanish, the Mexicans, and later the Americans would find this independence of action and decentralized political structure difficult to comprehend.

The wickiup, a traditional Apache home, is a dome-shaped structure made from a frame of flexible oak and willow poles with brush and hides thrown on top of it.

Among the Apache, proper rules of behavior were especially important when dealing with the dead. If an Apache died at home, the relatives made a hole in the wall of the *wickiup*, a dome-shaped dwelling place covered in hides, and removed the body. Then they destroyed the wickiup as well as the person's possessions. From that time forward, the family strictly avoided mentioning the dead person by name, although they could refer to the deceased indirectly. The Apache believed that even casual contact with the dead might draw the ghost to the living, often with perilous results. "Ghost sickness," unless treated, could result in death for an unlucky Apache.

The counterpart to these beliefs concerning death was a personal emphasis on attaining long life and good health. Reliance on family members and faith in leaders was not enough, however. The

Apache sought aid from other-than-human forces in the universe, just as Child of the Water had done in his quest to rid the world of monsters. Often appearing as an animal or some natural feature like a cloud, these forces reached out to a human and offered assistance and guidance in return for ceremonial offerings of prayer and respect. The Apache shaman and war leader Geronimo, for instance, often called on his power to extricate his band from difficult situations. On one such occasion, it is told, he delayed the onset of dawn so his people could escape under cover of darkness. As one of his followers, interviewed by the anthropologist Morris Opler for his 1941 study *An Apache Lifeway*, recalled, "He wanted morning to break after we had climbed over a mountain, so that the enemy couldn't see us. So Geronimo sang, and the night remained for two or three hours longer. I saw this myself."

Guidance and protection also came from the knowledge inherent in the land itself. Over generations of residence, the Apache built up a collection of stories intimately associated with what they now considered their homelands. Geographic features such as Mescal Mountain in Arizona figured in Apache stories of the beginning, in this case the place where the birds and other good animals, tired of perpetual night, gambled for daylight with the animals that favored the dark. The victory of the birds allowed daylight into the world, bringing light, warmth, and comfort. Mountains in particular never ceased their hold on the Apache, becoming almost like kin, taking an interest in Apache safety. When Chiricahua Apache warriors returned from their raids, they referred to the first mountains they saw by a special term that literally meant the mountains were looking for them, telling them that home was near. Other features of the landscape figured in stories of people who had strayed from proper behavior toward selfishness or wickedness. And so the sight of a butte or a stream, like an esteemed elderly relative telling a story to impart a moral, might remind the Apache to live their lives properly lest they too succumb to misfortune.

As the Apache entered the seventeenth and eighteenth centuries, they encountered another people, the Spanish, who told different kinds of stories about the mountains and the plains. These people imagined a "New Mexico," a new empire of Indian peoples subject to the Spanish Crown to rival the conquered Aztec realms to the south. Eventually, however, they would come to accept a world partly on Apache terms.

Changes from
the South

Vivorá and Tetsegoslán grumbled. Who was El Compá to think he was the "Principal Chief of the Apache," even if the Spanish commandant said he was. El Compá held out his hands. Of course he was not the principal chief. The Apache knew no such person. But the Spanish were a foolish people. Better to humor them. Besides, today the Spanish promised something special. "Would we still receive our cigarettes?" Tetsegoslán's wife asked. "Yes, yes, of course," El Compá replied. "And corn and sugar and salt as usual. Meat too. And I have asked for chocolate and candy for the little ones. But there is more; trust me and come to the fort."

The Apache gathered outside the walls of the little fort at Janos in Mexico. El Compá was right. The soldiers stood by piles of shoes and hats, trousers and colorful ribbons, even earrings, beads, and buttons. Men and women tried on this hat or that, passing them around, laughing when Juan Diego, El Compá's son, put on a jacket much too large for him. The Spanish captain smiled, too. "That jacket is for your father. He is a good man and a friend to the Spanish." El Compá was pleased. Even Vivorá and Tetsegoslán praised El Compá, for they had received many serapes and saddle blankets, as well as muskets and shot.

Then the Spanish captain spoke. Your brothers the Mescalero steal the horses and cattle at Paso del Norte. We have tried to make peace with them but they refuse. They refuse our gifts. Will you help us? The headmen considered. "I will not go," Vivorá said. "My wives need to gather mescal." The captain turned to Tetsegoslán. The Apache leader nodded to his brother, Jasquieljal, whom the Spanish called El Padre. Yes, he would go. But he would keep anything recovered from the Mescalero. "All except the cattle and horses," agreed the captain. "They must go back to their owners." El Padre looked at the other Apache. Who would journey to El Norte with him?

Later that day, five warriors, eight women, and a boy, learning the ways of raid and war, rode north with a company of Spanish troops.

Chocolate, saddle blankets, shoes, hats, beads, and buttons all point to significant material changes in the Apache way of life. Yet the episode at Janos points to other cultural changes influenced by contact with the Spanish. The Apache now had horses and guns. Some Apache lived peacefully near Spanish forts and accepted Spanish gifts. Others ran off with Spanish cattle and horses. Clearly much had changed in the Apache world.

A "NEW MEXICO" AND A "NEW WORLD"

The Spanish considered the Coronado expedition of the 1540s a failure. The Querechos were not the wealthy, powerful Aztec, who could be conquered and converted for the greater glory of crown and church, nor did the mountains and plains seem hospitable to settlement. Later expeditions confirmed this view, adding that mineral wealth was not to be found either. Nevertheless, the Spanish established a "New Mexico," a new province largely dedicated to the conversion of the village-dwelling Pueblo Indians to Catholicism. As the Spanish launched their missionary effort among the Pueblo villagers of the Rio Grande Valley in the first three-quarters of the seventeenth century, the Apache continued their east/west split. Following the Pueblo Indians' own orientation, the Spanish initially found themselves trading with the eastern Apache, who still came to the Pueblo villages to trade their meat and hides.

The eastern Apache readily expanded their trade to incorporate the Spanish, who introduced a variety of new products and trade items, including cloth, beads, and metal objects like knives and awls. In many ways these objects made life easier and were quickly adapted by men and women. Soon trade contacts increased, and Spanish records speak of Apache trading parties coming to the Pueblo villages with hundreds of dogs, groaning under packs of hides and meat. Through trade came other cultural influences on the Apache as well. One group of Apache, called *Jicarillas* or "little basket makers" by the Spanish, even settled for a time in semipermanent villages near the pueblo of Taos, living in adobe houses and practicing irrigated farming. There they adopted other Pueblo cultural traits, including the use of corn in particular rituals. More generally, other Apache incorporated some degree of gardening into their lives, although agriculture never became as central to their economic, social, or ceremonial life as it did among the various Pueblo groups.

Increased contact with the Spanish also led to raiding. Such was the availability of cattle and corn and other products in the Pueblo and Spanish villages that some Apache began to take what they wanted. Spanish and Pueblo villages experienced Apache raids to such an extent that even peaceful Apache trading parties were forced by their Pueblo hosts to spend the night outside of their villages as a precaution. Raiding also brought other kinds of goods into the trade system, most notably human slaves. The Spanish and even the Pueblos used captives as labor in their mining or agricultural tasks, and the Apache responded in kind. Pawnee and Wichita villages to the east of the Apache of the high plains found themselves subject to raids, and hundreds of their people were transferred to New Mexico and points farther south. Even Apache became caught up in Spanish slave raids, becoming human commodities themselves.

As raiding developed throughout the seventeenth and eighteenth centuries, it became as important to Apache men as hunting. And like hunting, the Apache developed distinct sets of raiding practices. When a local leader voiced the need for more supplies, experienced men came forward to organize a raiding party. Other Apache responded, drawn by the expectations of rewards. For the most part, raids were nonconfrontational; Apache prized stealth and cunning, achieving their goals with minimal casualties. This was partly because raiding parties often included novices, and their families wished their young men to return home safely.

For young Apache men, raiding became a kind of rite of passage, a successful transition into adulthood. Older adult male relatives introduced an Apache boy to raiding about the age of sixteen. During raiding expeditions, the boy occupied himself with such camp tasks as gathering water, cooking food, or serving as a lookout. He followed certain ritual behaviors, including never touching water to his lips but drinking through a straw, and learned a specialized raiding vocabulary. In addition, his mentors referred to him as "Child of the Water," underscoring the importance of his preparation for adulthood. During this time, the adults shielded the boy from physical danger, more concerned with broadening his experience, testing his physical endurance, and developing his patience. Upon the completion of four raids, the boy was considered a man and could organize raiding parties of his own.

Despite their precautions, the Apache sometimes experienced casualties. Then a family would organize a war dance to persuade others to join a revenge party. Morris Opler published one such account in his book *An Apache Lifeway*. The war dance, his informant explained, "means that they are going after all their enemies. . . . It doesn't have to be the ones that killed their men. They go after anything. . . . They fight anyone to get even." As Spaniards and Pueblo Indians sought to protect themselves from Apache raids or as they in turn retaliated for past Apache raids, revenge-motivated warfare increased on both sides, prompting Spanish policymakers on the frontier and back in Mexico City to give much thought as to how to break this vicious cycle.

One item that the Apache increasingly acquired in raids was the horse, which would profoundly affect Plains Indian life. Historian Elliott West has likened the introduction of the horse to the "grass revolution." That is, horses allowed people to tap into the enormous stores of solar energy locked up in the vast grasslands of the plains. Grasses powered horses, and horses in turn opened up the great buffalo herds to an extent never before possible. Buffalo robes and hides poured into the waiting hands of European traders—not only the Spanish, but also soon the French and later the English, operating from the middle Missouri River Valley. Although these developments gave Apache the incentive to break from the mountains and move more permanently onto the plains, they faced increased competition from other Native peoples. In particular, the Shoshonean-speaking Comanche, with access to firearms acquired in trade with the French, became the horse-mounted masters of the central plains by the mid-eighteenth century, throwing the Apache back toward New Mexico and west Texas. Now the Comanche came to dominate the great Pueblo trading fairs, arriving with hundreds of horses laden with robes, hides, and meat, driving slaves before them. In exchange they received corn, sugar, horses, mules, knives, hatchets, tobacco, and myriad other products. Recognizing the shift in power alignments, Spanish officials by the last quarter of the eighteenth century sought to ally with the Comanche in order to curb Apache raiding and warfare. Horses, then, never quite transformed the Apache into true Plains Indians, as they did for the Comanche, the Cheyenne, and the Lakota. Nevertheless, eastern Apache took to horses to increase their access to the buffalo, darting out from the mountains into the plains and then back again.

The western segment of the Apache nation remained outside of the immediate sphere of the Spanish settlements. However, evidence seems to point to their gradual movement westward and southward, where eventually they would differentiate into the historic Chiricahua, Mescalero, Western Apache, and Navajo peoples (traditionally scholars consider the Navajo separately from the Apache; heavily influenced by the Pueblo Indians and the Spanish, Navajo life and culture developed in different directions from their Apache relatives). Like their eastern relatives, the western segment of the Apache increasingly took to raiding, turning their attention to the developing livestock industry of northern New Spain. Striking from their camps in southern New Mexico and Arizona, small groups of Apache raiders descended on Spanish ranches, running off cattle and horses, using both for food.

COPING WITH RAIDING AND WARFARE

The rise of Apache raiding unsettled northern New Spain, which had been racked by Indian revolts since the 1680s when the Pueblo peoples briefly expelled the Spanish from New Mexico. With French and English interlopers adding to the unrest, Spanish officials set out to win back control of the north, part of a much larger effort to reinvigorate the Spanish colonies in general. By the last quarter of the eighteenth century, Spanish military officials worked tirelessly to establish or relocate presidios or forts,

Bernardo de Galvez, viceroy of New Spain, offered the Apache food, shelter, and agricultural training in an effort to curb raids on Spanish settlements. Encouraged to become dependent on Spanish handouts, the Apache soon assimilated into the Spanish way of life.

The Compá Family

If the peace establishment program had operated according to plan, most Apache would have followed the trajectory of the Compá family. Most closely connected with the presidio of Janos, the Compás maintained a relationship with the Spanish and then the Mexicans from the 1790s through the 1830s. The father, El Compá, may have reasoned that cooperation with the Spanish not only enhanced his status but also brought material rewards to himself and his kin group. At one point, for his services, El Compá received a Spanish-style house in Janos and his wives received extra daily rations of half a sheep. At other times, he intervened for his relatives with the Spanish, undoubtedly cementing his role as a headman in their eyes. Certainly he was the "headman" in the estimation of the Spanish, who in 1791 styled him "principal chief of the Apache at peace."

upgrade garrisons, and train militia. From these presidios, soldiers set out to punish Apache raiders and recover Spanish possessions, sometimes in concert with new Comanche allies, now establishing their dominance over the southern plains against all rivals.

By the 1790s Spanish soldiers began to understand the nature of Apache raiding and warfare, realizing that indiscriminate warfare antagonized relatively peaceful groups accidentally caught up in Spanish reprisals. Now field commanders made every effort to punish only identified raiding parties (different "brands" of cigarettes disbursed to Apache groups, for instance, allowed the Spanish to track the movements of raiding parties). This limited the number of Apache who might participate in a revenge raid.

On El Compá's death in 1794, one of his sons, Juan Diego, took over his father's role as headman. Incomplete Spanish records make it difficult to follow Juan Diego fully, but he and his family figure prominently as the recipients of special gifts from the Spanish. When Juan Diego claimed the title of "principal chief," however, other Apache leaders complained and the commandant of the Janos presidio had to assure them that Juan Diego enjoyed no such status.

Another of El Compá's sons, Juan José, was the only Apache to attend the presidio school maintained for the sons of soldiers. Demonstrating a knack for handwriting, he was awarded a scholarship of a *peso* from the commandant. In the 1830s, Juan José's fluency in Spanish made him an important mediator between Apache and Mexican authorities attempting to reinstitute the peace establishment program, which was shut down earlier because of increasing costs. Given the title "General of the Apache," Juan José exerted little of the influence of his father, as worsening Mexican-Apache relations undermined opportunities for peace.

Likewise, the Spanish military limited "revenge raids" undertaken by ordinary Spanish settlers by requiring a pass for travel. Finally, commanders initiated strict supervision of trade encounters to prevent cheating of the Apache, thereby reducing the likelihood of retaliatory raids.

The ultimate goal of these measures was to change Apache behavior and, over time, Apache culture. As Viceroy Bernardo de Gálvez remarked in his famous *Instructions* to military commanders, "They [the Apache] should be made accustomed to the use of our foods, drinks, arms, and clothing, and they should become greedy for the possession of land." He continued, "Even if in the beginning we are not successful in achieving these ends, as they require much time, this course will put us on the path to eventual success." Trade contacts alone, however, would not achieve these ends. Apache headmen must receive regular gifts and their people access to food, urged Gálvez, and only in this way could they be persuaded to give up raiding. Translating recommendations into policy, military officials quickly turned a number of presidios into "peace establishments," places where the Apache would be encouraged to settle, receive rations, take up farming, learn Spanish ways, and eventually become productive citizens of northern New Spain. By 1793, eight peace establishments (six attached to presidios) harbored some 2,000 Apache.

Peace establishments, however, never brought about the profound cultural transformation of the Apache that Gálvez and other officials envisioned. Most Apache remained outside the orbit of the establishments, and those who settled there exercised great latitude in how they adopted to Spanish culture. Largely this resulted from the limits of Spanish military power (although sometimes Apache avoided the peace establishments because of outbreaks of smallpox or other diseases there). Stretched to the breaking point, the Spanish military could not compel the Apache to settle down. Instead, they had to entice them with gifts and regular distributions of rations. Rising administrative costs, however, led to modifications in the program. Initially encouraged to settle near the peace establishments and to seek passes to hunt or gather mescal, the Apache were soon encouraged to leave. To the exasperation of military officials, many Apache refused, loath to give up their access to gifts and rations.

The more ambitious parts of the peace establishment program, such as the adoption of farming or ranching, also made little headway. Unable to force the Apache to do anything, the Spanish hoped that some might prove interested in imitating the soldiers' farming or ranching tasks. However, those who showed some interest soon became diverted. In the same way, systematic religious instruction did not occur. Spanish priests baptized some individual Apache, but the majority remained aloof from Christianity. In fact, the military at times discouraged baptisms, arguing that conversion could not come without true understanding. Finally, education attempts on the whole proved disappointing. Peace establishments, then, functioned mainly as distribution centers for various material objects and rations rather than as dispensers of "civilization." Apache acquired cloth, clothes, knives, soap, sugar, salt, tobacco, corn, and, most importantly, meat in the disbursements. Indeed, when other rations were in short supply, officials gave no small effort to ensuring meat allotments. Subsequently, some Apache from the peace establishments recirculated many of these items in trade with other Apache outside the line of Spanish settlements.

Although raiding never entirely ceased during the rest of Spain's tenure, it decreased significantly, allowing population growth and economic revival, mainly in a "pacified" zone, approximately 90 miles (145 kilometers) north from the line of presidios that stretched across the frontier (roughly following today's U.S./Mexico border, with the New Mexican settlements stretching up like a finger). The Apache homelands remained largely outside of this zone. As a result, the Apache exercised considerable freedom in how they chose to respond to the Spanish, either through raids, simple avoidance, trading, or temporary residence at a peace establishment. For their part, the Spanish strictly modified their own behavior toward the Apache. Only by repeated example, enlightened discipline, and infinite patience, the Spanish reasoned, could the Apache be persuaded to forgo their "savagery" and embrace "civilization." What they did not realize was that the Apache had their own concept of "civilization."

Violence
over the Land

Juan José Compá, his brother Juan Diego, and the other Apache
leaders, Marcelo and Guero, led their people to the camp at
Dzisl-di-jole or "Round Mountain." There they could hunt, and
the women could gather plants. Also, water flowed in abundance,
providing drinks for thirsty Apache and horses.

Times had changed, however. Few peace establishments
welcomed the Apache, and those that did had little in the way
of gifts or food. Fewer Apache trusted Juan José or his brother,
accusing them of always making excuses for the Mexicans and
urging the Apache to make peace. Many Apache now took to
raiding, running off scores of cattle and mules, selling them to
the white men who asked few questions about the animals' ori-
gins. And now a group of white men approached the Apache
camp, making signs of friendship and indicating their willingness to trade.

For two days friendship and trade progressed, with Apache visiting the camp of the man called Johnson and his 17 companions. With them were five Mexicans, and Juan Diego could speak with them, acting as an interpreter during the good-natured haggling over goods and animals. On the third day, the Apache returned to Johnson's camp, but the Mexicans were gone. Nevertheless, Johnson and his men smiled and urged them to come forward to examine even more goods spread out on a blanket. In their eagerness, none of the Apache noticed Johnson signal to some men hiding behind the scrub. Suddenly they swiveled a small cannon into place and fired, sharp pieces of metal scraps flying into the flesh of Apache men, women, and children. And as one, Johnson's men brought forth rifles, concealed in their serapes, and began to fire into the crowd. Shocked and dazed, the survivors fled, leaving 20 dead behind, including the Compás, Marcelo, and Guero.

THE CONFLICT BEGINS

After a decade of revolution, Mexico achieved its independence from Spain in 1821. And just like the United States, Mexico faced profound financial, economic, and political challenges in its early years. The effect on the peace establishment program was immediate. Neither the Mexican states of Chihuahua and Sonora nor the new national government could afford the steady supply of gifts, rations, and regulated trade so necessary to its success. Soon Apache raids picked up in response all across the north. The western-oriented groups swept across Chihuahua and Sonora and soon brought southern New Mexico into their scope. Mescalero and Lipan Apache ranged along the northeast, raiding throughout Chihuahua, Coahuila, and Durango.

Although the demise of the peace establishment program contributed to the intensification in raiding, equally important was the market for stolen goods in trading posts set up just outside of Mexican territory by American merchant and fur-trading companies. Cattle, horses, and mules poured into these posts, while guns, ammunition, and other manufactured goods poured out, often making the Apache better armed than the inhabitants of northern Mexico. Even more important to the American traders were the more numerous Comanche, who continued their expansion on the southern plains, reaching into Texas and northern Mexico, driving off thousands of horses, mules, and livestock—mules in particular fetching the highest prices because they could be resold to the emerging cotton kingdom in the United States. The Comanche brought hundreds of captives north out of Mexico as well, captives who provided the labor force for their livestock herding and trade. Comanche success attracted other Native peoples to the southern plains, such as the Kiowa, who left their homes in the Black Hills and moved south of the Arkansas River, allying with the Comanche, increasing their strength even more. Joining the Kiowa, a small group of Apache took to the fully mounted plains way of life, becoming known as the Kiowa-Apache (sometimes called the Plains Apache), a small cog in the Comanche "empire."

DESPERATE MEASURES

Interviewing Apache for his 1941 book, *An Apache Lifeway*, anthropologist Morris Opler asked his informants about the taking of scalps. Almost to a person, they claimed that scalping originated with the Mexicans. "The Mexicans used to take scalps. They started it first," emphasized one informant, "before the Chiricahua." Another, while acknowledging the taking of scalps for ceremonial purposes, narrowed its incidence: "Scalping is used as a last resort on a man who has made a great deal of trouble for the Chiricahua. Such a man, when finally caught, would be scalped and 'danced on.' He was scalped after he was dead. The whole scalp was taken off. In the dance the pole is in the center with the scalp on top, and they dance around it." Significantly he added, "This is used mostly on Mexicans who did awful things against the Chiricahua."

Preserved in the historical memory of these Chiricahua Apache were the "scalp laws" of the 1830s and 1840s, enacted by the states of Chihuahua and Sonora. Unable to cope with Apache raids through conventional means, both states began to offer bounties for Apache scalps. Soon these laws and the money they promised attracted a host of "professional" and part-time bounty hunters to Mexico's north—many, like John Johnson and the notorious James Kirker, were foreigners. To maximize their profits, these men preferred to surprise large numbers of Apache, often during peaceful trading encounters. Indeed, using such tactics, Kirker and his men killed almost 500 Apache during their bloody career. Most of these "successes" came in the early phase of the bounty program, when it was still possible to catch Apache unaware. By the 1850s, scalp hunting proved more difficult as Apache leaders exercised extreme caution in dealing with non-Apache. As a result, the bounties increased. Kirker had received $50 for each scalp taken. When the German traveler Julius Froebel visited Chihuahua, the scale had increased four times: "[The government] has set a high reward for every Indian either captured or killed. It gives 200 dollars for every adult Indian, alive or dead. In the last case the scalp and ears of the victim must be exhibited in proof of the fact. An Indian woman, alive, is valued at 150 dollars; a living boy at the same sum, while for the one dead 100 dollars is given."

Among the Apache, the scalp hunting triggered revenge-motivated warfare as parties of aggrieved kin sought retribution, meting out violence across Mexico's northern frontier. To protect themselves from raids, many small Mexican communities entered into informal understandings with individual Apache groups. Called "partial peace treaties" by Mexican historian Francisco Almada, these understandings insulated a particular village from Apache raids if it agreed to serve as a clearinghouse for stolen livestock and other booty. Yet these same villages were often tempted to break the treaties in an effort to collect the bounty on Apache scalps. A young Apache, Jason Betzinez, described one such incident that occurred in 1850 at the small settlement of Ramos. The townspeople induced

Geronimo's Tragedy

War leader, shaman, prisoner of war, World's Fair exhibit—
Geronimo was probably the most famous Apache in the
late nineteenth and early twentieth centuries. At one point,
Geronimo and his followers led one-quarter of the United
States Army on a chase through the American Southwest and
northern Mexico. For many, his surrender in 1886 marked
the end of the last major American Indian war in the United
States. And yet, Geronimo's career, his rise to prominence or
notoriety, had its origin in the tragic deaths of his mother,
wife, and three children in the waning days of the peace establishments of northern Mexico.

In 1858 Colonel José María Carrasco, commandant of
Sonora, led 400 troops into the neighboring state of Chihuahua, where his forces descended on 180 Apache families
peacefully encamped near the presidio and former peace
establishment of Janos. Although other state officials had
concluded that the Janos Apache had not taken part in raids
throughout the region, Carrasco was determined to send a
message to all Apache. No longer would Apache raids be
tolerated, nor the growing contraband trade in stolen goods.
Carrasco divided his forces near Janos, and his men attacked

a group of Apache to enter the settlement to trade. There they plied
them with mescal (a strong liquor distilled from desert plants), and
soon the Apache returned to their camp to sleep off its effects. Then,
as recounted in *I Fought with Geronimo*,

> [j]ust before first light, Mexican soldiers and villagers slipped
> into the Indian camp. They carried ready muskets, spears,
> knives, and clubs. At a sudden signal violent firing broke out.
> Following this first ragged volley the stabbing and hacking and

the small Apache camps scattered throughout the vicinity. Next his men attacked the town itself, killing more Apache outside the presidio's walls. Geronimo's camp was attacked while most of the men were absent. In his official report, Carrasco claimed to have killed 16 men and 5 women and captured 62 more, most of them women and children. Casualties were undoubtedly higher than that reflected in Carrasco's report, for Geronimo alone lost his mother and his wife that day, as well as three of his children.

"I stood until all had passed, hardly knowing what I would do," Geronimo recalled in his autobiography. "I had no weapon, nor did I hardly wish to fight, neither did I contemplate recovering the bodies of my loved ones, for that was forbidden. I did not pray, nor did I resolve to do anything in particular, for I had no purpose left." Geronimo and the other survivors returned to Arizona where, according to Apache custom, he destroyed his family's belongings. His life would never be the same. "I was never again contented in our quiet home," he wrote. "True, I could visit my father's grave, but I had vowed vengeance upon the Mexican troopers who had wronged me, and whenever I came near his grave or saw anything to remind me of our former happy days my heart would ache for revenge upon Mexico."

clubbing of recumbent forms commenced. . . . In a short time most of the Indians were lying in their blood, dead or dying. The Mexicans fell to work with sharp knives, wrenching off the gory trophies for which they would receive gold and silver from the authorities.

Betzinez's grandfather, Tudeevia, who probably told the young man this story, participated in an unusually large revenge expedition launched some months later. One hundred seventy-five

When the peace between Mexico and the Apache ended, raiding resumed once again and the Mexican government began offering a bounty for every Apache scalp. Geronimo, a famous Apache warrior, lost five members of his family in a Mexican raid and vowed to have revenge.

warriors and apprentices took part, including rising Apache leaders such as Cochise and Geronimo.

WAR UPON WAR

In 1846 the United States and Mexico went to war, sparked by the American annexation of the former Mexican province of Texas. As American troops marched into Mexico's north, they received their first glimpses of a land already devastated by nearly 15 years of Apache and Comanche raiding and warfare. Abandoned homes, farms, and ranches dotted the landscape. Refugees flocked to the towns, which American troops found crowded with exhausted men, women, and children. In fact, U.S. president James K. Polk and his advisers had counted on this dire situation to counter northern Mexican resistance to the American invasion. The government instructed military commanders to inform the people that they came as liberators and protectors and that soon the Apache and Comanche would be brought to heel.

When war finally ended in 1848, the Treaty of Guadalupe Hidalgo between the United States and Mexico made this promise explicit. In addition to the transfer of vast lands to the victorious Americans, the treaty bound the United States to prevent raiding south of the new international boundary and to rescue Mexican captives held by the Apache, Comanche, and other tribes. Yet, by now, raiding was a well-established cultural practice and generated products and commodities essential to the economic and social well-being of both peoples. Young Apache men, for example, eager to demonstrate their worthiness as potential marriage partners to their future in-laws, approached a young woman's family with gifts, most often a horse or horses. As an informant explained in Morris Opler's *An Apache Lifeway*:

> We do this because a woman is more valuable than a man. We do it to accommodate the woman. The son-in-law is considered a son and as one of the family. The in-laws depend a great deal on him. They depend on him for hunting and all kinds of

work. . . . In return he has privileges with the property of his wife's people. He can get anything they have very easily. It is understood that he can call on them for aid.

Raiding also produced captives, increasingly important as warfare, disease, and other factors depleted Apache numbers. As another Chiricahua Apache informant described the situation in *An Apache Lifeway*:

> Grown men are never kept alive to be married into the tribe or enslaved. A mature man is dangerous, and they kill him. But a young boy of four, five, or six is adopted into the tribe. He becomes a real Chiricahua [Apache] and later marries into the tribe. Children like this are captured when their father and mother are killed. The Chiricahua take the children to increase the tribe, and they are treated like other children. When the Chiricahua attack a village, they don't kill the women and children much, but let them run away.

For the time being, American policymakers underestimated the enormity of the task before them. Raiding and warfare and the taking of captives were not practices that could be ended with the wave of a hand. American military and government officials would have to reach out to numerous Apache groups—the Chiricahua bands straddling the international border at the intersection of New Mexico, Arizona, and Chihuahua; the Western Apache groups north and west of the Chiricahua; the Mescalero and Jicarilla in southeastern and northeastern New Mexico; the Lipan in parts of Texas; and the Kiowa-Apache following their Kiowa sponsors throughout the southern plains—and try to impress upon them the American promises to Mexico.

Yet the plight of captives and the ongoing raids into Mexico failed to capture the imagination of the average American. Gold fever struck the United States in 1849 as stories of rivers flowing with gold swept out of the newly acquired California. Soon, thousands began the long trek westward to make their fortunes.

To these and others interested in reaching California, the question was how to get there in the fastest and safest way possible, and many looked to the government to provide safe passage. As most routes involved traveling through American Indian territory, it was a question that concerned scores of Indian nations, including the Apache, and soon occupied much of the government's attention.

ROADS THROUGH THE WEST

Determined to protect American citizens on their immigration to California and other western territories, the United States negotiated two important treaties in the early 1850s that created broad corridors through Indian country, with military posts along the routes to protect both immigrants and Indians. The government further pledged to supply tribes with annuities or annual distributions of payments (often in the form of goods). The Treaty of Fort Laramie dealt with tribes of the northern plains, the Treaty of Fort Atkinson the southern.

Tellingly, Mexican captives, conversant in Spanish and Comanche and other Plains Indian languages, played a role in interpreting the Treaty of Fort Atkinson's terms, which included the familiar pledge to end raids into Mexico and to restore captives. Although these pledges were important to the government, few of the tribes seemed to have regarded them as of great consequence. The Kiowa, for one, did not note the treaty as a significant event on their winter count, a calendar device used by several Plains tribes to mark important happenings. Nevertheless, the implications of the treaty directly affected many Indian nations, including the Kiowa-Apache.

As more immigrants crossed through the plains, they disrupted the Indian way of life in many ways. Immigrant wagons cut deep ruts into the plains, their oxen and mules fouled watercourses and ate their way through the native grasses. Immigrants cut stands of scarce timber used by the Indian peoples for fuel or

Settlers heading to the West and Southwest were in constant danger, as they traveled on rough lands, in unpredictable climate, and under threat of Native American raiding parties. In an attempt to protect its citizens, the U.S. government signed peace treaties with the Apache and other groups.

the construction of their lodges. In the vicinity of the long wagon trains, game became scarce and hunting more difficult. Most frightening, immigrants brought diseases. In 1849, for example, Kiowa and Kiowa-Apache participating in a Sun Dance, an important ritual of spiritual renewal among the Plains tribes, were struck by cholera, apparently contracted from a group of forty-niners (as gold seekers were called) on their way to California. So feared was the disease, which killed its victims through severe dehydration, that several Kiowa and Kiowa-Apache people took their own lives, choosing a speedy death on their own terms. The rest, panicked, scattered into the plains, leaving their belongings and lodges abandoned.

Farther to the west and south, Mescalero and Jicarilla Apache also saw an influx of forty-niners, although not in the numbers using the trails over the plains. However, they faced many of the same issues as their Plains Indian cousins. As on the plains, the American military began to establish posts throughout Apache country, competing with the Apache for the best range lands and water and attracting settlers eager to sell needed materials to the army. One such settler, E.J. White, traveling to Fort Buchanan, was caught up in a revenge raid of Jicarilla Apache, themselves provoked by a senseless attack earlier by soldiers in Las Vegas, New Mexico. He was killed, and his wife and child were captured. A hastily formed posse pursued and overtook the raiders, but White's wife and child were already dead. Members of the posse swore revenge then and there, feeding a growing cycle of raids and counterraids. In Arizona, Chiricahua Apache also watched as immigrants followed the trails, in this case to the southeast, as disappointed gold seekers from California came to Arizona hoping to find the next big bonanza. Some of these settlers reached their own private understandings with the Apache, similar to the "partial peace treaties" in Mexico. In this case, they turned a blind eye to continuing raids into Mexico as long as they were unmolested or could buy some of the booty from south of the border. Meanwhile, the United States Army Corps of Topographical Engineers scoured the Southwest and the plains, exploring possible routes for a transcontinental railroad to California.

To the citizens of Mexico, however, all this activity did little to stem Indian raids south of the border, and soon claims for compensation reached Washington at an alarming rate. In 1854, the American government took the opportunity of a new treaty with Mexico, the Gadsden Purchase agreement, which procured additional Mexican lands south of the Gila River for a railroad route, to

settle all claims with Mexico and to relieve itself of further obligations to protect Mexican citizens or rescue Mexican captives. Yet,
the situation was far from settled. The lands newly acquired from
Mexico were part of Apache territory, and some sort of understanding would have to be reached with the Chiricahua and other
Apache.

Resistance

The Mexicans drove the Apache women forward, 200 miles (320 kilometers) through the cactus and scrub on their way to the Gulf of California. Once at the coast, the Mexicans herded them aboard a ship that would take them to a life of servitude in a penal colony far to the south in Baja California. Many died from disease and maltreatment, but Dilchthe survived, determined to escape and rejoin her daughter and grandchildren far off in the Black Mountains of New Mexico. One night as the guards slept, Dilchthe and the remaining women fled into the night. Hiding by day, they slowly moved along the coast, ever northward toward the Colorado River, where they could finally turn east toward their home. Weeks passed as they walked and walked, bruised and footsore, subsisting on little more than seeds and insects, over the strange and unfamiliar land.

Finally they came to the place where the two rivers met—the wide and deep Colorado and the smaller Gila River. Some of the women despaired of crossing, but Dilchthe reminded them that they were Apache and boldly waded into the muddy waters. Deeper and deeper rose the water, but never above her armpits, and soon she waded out onto the other side. The other women followed. Exhausted, all rested before resuming their long trek. Three days out from the river, however, disaster struck. Mojave Indians attacked. Only Dilchthe and one other woman escaped.

Still they trudged on and on, now into the vast and waterless desert, tired beyond endurance and near starvation. Too exhausted to continue, they fell to the ground. Eventually the morning haze lifted. Dilchthe pushed herself up and squinted into the light as a heart-shaped mountain slowly emerged. "I know of only one place" cried Dilchthe, "where there is a mountain shaped like that one—in our own home country." Calling on the last of her strength, she gathered wood and sticks to build a small smoky fire, hoping that other Apache might investigate.

The two Apache men were out hunting when they noticed the smoke. They moved cautiously forward and saw the two women, almost dead from starvation. Suddenly one of the men ran forward. Here was his wife's mother, Dilchthe, captured by the Mexicans and long given up for lost. Joyfully he embraced her, giving her water to drink and food to eat. His companion stiffened, for an Apache man avoided his mother-in-law as a sign of respect. Yet then he relaxed and smiled. Her son-in-law had saved her life. He had not only shown her respect but love as well.

THE CHIRICAHUA APACHE EXPERIENCE

As the nineteenth century progressed, the Apache faced growing pressure from the United States and Mexico. By the 1880s both countries had embarked on modernization of their frontiers, building railroads and developing agricultural and mineral resources. New population appeared, competing with the Apache and other Native peoples for land. Where Mexico's north met the American West, the Apache found their homelands shrinking as the militaries of two countries forced them onto reservations.

The homelands of the Chiricahua Apache straddled the U.S.-Mexico border. Specifically, the people lived in bands in southeastern Arizona, southwestern New Mexico, and the adjacent regions of Mexico. So situated, Chiricahua raiders operated throughout a broad area of the Southwest and northern Mexico. Yet the history of the Chiricahua demonstrated that the people could live at peace as well. The Compás, for example, who worked to solidify relations between the Spanish and the Apache at the peace establishments, were Chiricahua, as was Mangas Coloradas, a principal leader who earlier had signaled his willingness to work with the Americans in the late 1840s and 1850s. Relations with Mexico, however, remained sour, exacerbated by scalp hunting and the Apache desire for revenge.

Early efforts at establishing peaceful Chiricahua and American relations, however, faced a variety of difficulties. First, little cooperation existed between the U.S. military and the Office of Indian Affairs (later the Bureau of Indian Affairs), which dispatched so-called Indian agents to reach out to tribal groups and establish reservations. Both groups believed their methods of regulation superior and constantly criticized each other in official correspondence sent back to Washington. Moreover, neither group fully understood the dynamics of Apache culture, especially the limits of chiefly authority. Important leaders like Cochise or Mangas Coloradas relied on persuasion and experience in dealing with their people, but their words of counsel did not bind other Apache bands or tribes. As a result, a series of incidents occurred that threatened to poison Apache and American relations from the start. At one point, for instance, an overzealous army officer, Lieutenant George Bascom, arrested the important Chiricahua leader Cochise, holding him responsible for raids conducted by the Western Apache. Cochise escaped, but in the conflict that followed, he lost his brother and

Tensions between the U.S. military and Native Americans through-out the United States were quickly escalating into violence. Cochise (*above*), chief of the Chiricahua Apache, was accused of conducting raids. When he escaped arrest, members of his family were killed.

two nephews. When Mangas Coloradas attempted to broker a peace two years later, a detachment of troops tortured the old chief and later killed him as he was "trying to escape." In a final act of treachery, another group of soldiers mutilated the chief's body.

A second difficulty in laying the groundwork for peace was the growing presence of non-Apache throughout Arizona. The discovery of gold in the territory, the growing evidence of copper deposits, and the opportunities for ranching brought more settlers to the area. Few showed respect for prior Apache claims to the land or for the peacemaking efforts, such as they were, of Indian agents and the military. In 1871, for example, a so-called Committee of Public Safety in Tucson, made up of local whites, Mexicans, and Tohono O'odham Indians, descended on a peaceful encampment of Apache near Camp Grant, taking the lives of more than 100, mostly women and children. Although many victims of the Camp Grant massacre were Western Apache, the Chiricahua believed that such could be their fate if they trusted white promises of peace.

In the wake of the Camp Grant massacre, however, the federal government realized that new humanitarian approaches to the Chiricahua and other Apache would have to be implemented to win their confidence. Vincent Colyer, a representative of the Office of Indian Affairs, and later General O.O. Howard, a one-armed veteran of the Civil War, entered into negotiations with Cochise and his leading men, eventually emerging with an agreement acceptable to many Apache. Working with Indian agent Tom Jeffords, who would coordinate the disbursement of food, clothing, and other supplies, Cochise and his band would manage their own affairs on a 55-square-mile (142-square-kilometer) reservation that encompassed the Chiricahua and Dragoon Mountains. For his part, Cochise promised to end raiding and to protect the overland stage that ran through the new reservation.

In 1872, the new Chiricahua Reservation began auspiciously and soon attracted other Apache, including southern and eastern Chiricahua from Mexico and New Mexico. As raiding declined throughout the region, the reservation's success seemed assured. Problems, however, soon arose. Jeffords, crippled by an inadequate budget, found it difficult to procure and disburse regular rations to the Chiricahua, a problem familiar on reservations throughout the Southwest. This partly stemmed from budgetary problems in Washington and partly from corruption, as "rings" of ranchers, lawyers, and businessmen filled government supply contracts with substandard goods. In response, Chiricahua raids into Mexico stepped up, particularly as the reservation's southern boundary lay along the U.S.-Mexico border. Although Article 11 of the Gadsden Purchase agreement had absolved the United States of further responsibility for Indian raids into Mexico, American officials found the situation embarrassing, more so as formal Mexican complaints streamed into Washington. Military officials quickly seized on the situation to argue that more forceful means of Apache control were necessary, brushing aside Cochise's explanation that raids into Mexico were an entirely separate matter and one over which he had little control.

Against this backdrop, policymakers began to discuss ideas of relocation and concentration for the Apache, citing arguments of cost-effectiveness, expediency, and more effective, centralized control. Although an earlier experiment in Apache concentration had ended in disaster—the forced relocation of Mescalero Apache and Navajo to the Bosque Redondo region along the Pecos River in southeastern New Mexico—the federal government moved ahead with definite plans, dissolving the Chiricahua Reservation in 1876 and ordering the removal of its inhabitants to the San Carlos Reservation, away from the border and near the old Camp Grant. By 1878, more than 5,000 Apache, primarily Chiricahua and Western Apache from reservations throughout Arizona and New Mexico, found themselves sharing this new reservation home.

SAN CARLOS

In many ways, San Carlos represented a shrinking of the Chiricahua world. Whereas before local groups of extended families under a headman and respected elders determined where to hunt or camp, when to participate in raids, or when to gather mescal, now the military and later the civilian Indian agents gathered the people for daily roll calls and required permits for hunting, gathering, or travel on or off the reservation. With their movements curtailed, Apache depended on rations issued by the reservation's agent more than ever before. As a result, much activity centered on the agency headquarters, a few small adobe

The U.S. government forced several Apache groups to live on the San Carlos Reservation, a small area of land in Arizona. At San Carlos, the Apache were unable to travel in search of their own food and became dependent on government-issued rations.

buildings on the gravelly land between the sluggish San Carlos and Gila rivers, even though the reservation itself encompassed more than 7,000 square miles (18,000 square kilometers). In the flat desert country, away from the cool mountains, the Apache endured oppressive dust storms and heat, brackish water, and incessant mosquitoes and other pests. Agents used the disbursement of weekly rations as a means of control, and Apache received a monotonous diet of beef, flour, coffee, and salt, a far cry from fresh deer or horse meat, sweet mescal, wild greens, and parched corn.

Reservation agents, particularly the 22-year-old John Clum, who took over the position in 1874, considered rations but a temporary stage in Apache life; the people would learn how to be self-supporting, not through the life of hunting and gathering that had served the Apache for millennia, but through integration into a cash economy and the adoption of white farming methods. Under Clum's direction, Apache men embarked on an ambitious building program, constructing new agency headquarters, including living quarters for Clum and reservation employees, an office, a dispensary, blacksmith and carpenter shops, corrals, stalls, and a guardhouse for those who violated reservation rules. For their labor, Apache men received 50 cents a day, payable in reservation scrip, paper money issued in denominations of 50 cents, 25 cents, and 12.5 cents, redeemable only at the agency store.

Farming practices also underwent change. Those Apache who practiced some agriculture usually prepared only small plots, cultivated and cared for by women. Often planting corn, beans, and squash in one plot, women watched as the beans used the corn stalks for support and the squash spread along the ground, shaded by the corn. One plot then used little water, yielded a variety of food, and, more importantly, returned vital nutrients to the ground. Clum, on the other hand, had Apache men dig irrigation ditches to bring water to larger fields of one crop, such as barley. The agency would then buy the harvest, again using reservation scrip. A number of Apache gave Clum's farming methods a chance, but many more, recognizing their unsuitability in the hardscrabble desert, resisted his innovations and remained aloof.

Clum also interfered with traditional Apache means of leadership. Although he claimed that Apache would be governing themselves at San Carlos, he appointed a new force of Apache police and established an Apache court, with himself as chief justice. Those who cooperated with him, such as the Western Apache chief Eskiminzin, were singled out for praise as examples of "reformed" Apache. Those who resisted, such as the Eastern Chiricahua chief Victorio, who served a short while as a reservation judge only to quit in disgust as conditions on the reservation worsened, were denounced for their stubbornness. To most Apache, however, Clum was the stubborn one, a young man acting beyond his years, showing little respect for the authority and wisdom that came with age and proven leadership. In their language, they called him "Turkey Gobbler," always strutting about and putting himself forward.

The Apache tried to cope with San Carlos in different ways. Some cooperated with Clum, hoping to shield their people from the worst effects of the new regime. Others tried to adopt new activities to traditional roles, volunteering as Indian police or later as scouts for the army. Others, however, advocated escape, pointing to Mexico and the southern Chiricahua as an example of a still free Apache people. Among these Apache, Geronimo emerged as the leader of the final resistance to the reservation future.

THE FINAL RESISTANCE

Those Chiricahua who escaped from the reservation faced great personal hardship and sacrifice. Often separated from family and friends, they lived a life constantly on the run, traveling by night

Apache Women: Defenders of the People

All Apache valued the vast store of knowledge controlled by women. Apache women knew what plants provided strength and nourishment to maintain healthy families. They knew how to prepare game animals and make use of their hides for clothing and shelter. They read the landscape, noting the telltale signs of water or mescal ready for harvest. Many women accompanied their husbands on raids, tending camp and preparing food with the assistance of young novice warriors. When an Apache man took a bride and went to live with his wife's family, he showed special regard for his mother-in-law, to the point of never directly confronting her, keeping himself back, respectful and attentive.

During the long Chiricahua resistance, Apache women continued in these roles and took on new ones. Apache men often relied on their women to act as mediators, sending them out

and hiding by day, moving stealthily from mountain range to mountain range, trying to avoid the militaries of two countries intent on capturing or killing them. More and more, these Apache fixated on the territory of the southern Chiricahua leader, Juh, whose people lived immediately west of the Sonora-Chihuahua line in the Sierra Madre range of Mexico. The young Apache James Kaywaykla remembered his paternal grandfather describing Juh's mountain retreat: "[It] is an immense flat-topped mountain upon which there is a forest, streams, grass, and an abundance of game. To the top is one trail and only one. It is a zigzag path, leading to the crest." It was an area, his grandfather stressed, readily defensible. Along the path to the crest, Juh's people had placed huge stones that could be rolled down upon invaders. "[These stones] would sweep before them everything—invaders, stones, trees, to signal their willingness to trade with Mexican villagers or parley with American troops. These activities could be quite dangerous, as sometimes villagers captured Apache women, sending them into lives of enforced servitude. Favorite Apache stories concerned resourceful women who escaped captivity and under great odds managed to return to their people. If necessary, Apache women could fight too, knowing how to use knife, lance, and bow.

Like all Apache, women established relations with power, that all-encompassing force that permeated the Apache world, manifesting through natural forces or animal helpers. Some women drew on power for healing or to escape injuries, others to find food or shelter. Chief Victorio's sister Lozen, whose prowess as a warrior matched any man's, also drew on her power to locate enemies, providing valuable assistance to her brother on numerous occasions. Many Apache believe her absence from camp in 1879 allowed Mexican troops to ambush her people, leading to her brother's death.

earth. Mexican troops tried it once. There are still bits of metal and bones at the foot." Nana, James Kaywaykla's maternal grandfather, voiced similar thoughts. "He spoke," Kaywaykla recalled, "of how we might live indefinitely even if the trail were destroyed and we were cut off from all the rest of the world. We would be as those who are gone to the Happy Place of the Dead—provided with all necessities, protected from all enemies."

Yet Mexico, these Apache soon learned, provided little in the way of refuge. Mexican militia scoured the countryside looking for Apache camps. They dispatched captured men, women, and children to penal colonies in the south of the country, with some ending up as workers on henequen plantations in the Yucatán Peninsula. Others, particularly Apache women and children, became domestic servants, attached to the families that operated

After a successful military campaign against the Snake Indians in the Pacific Northwest, General George Crook (*above, on mule*) was reassigned to Arizona and the Apache Wars. Crook used fellow Apache to help track down runaways such as Geronimo.

the large farms and ranches that dotted the north of the country. Even other Apache joined the hunt for the Chiricahua runaways, recruited by General George Crook for their knowledge of the country and their stamina and endurance. These men believed further resistance was harmful to the Apache, as families lost loved ones to death or separation. These scouts, formed into companies of 25 under the leadership of one or two white officers, would cross the border into Mexico, pursuing Geronimo and his followers into the vast mountain ranges of northern Mexico, a fact that angered Mexican authorities who did not consider Apache scouts as "American troops."

By this time Mexican troops had already killed and scattered Victorio's followers. The great southern leader Juh had died in a tragic accident, leaving his young sons orphaned. With scouts on his trail and Mexican troops everywhere, Geronimo sensed his time was short and bowed to the wishes of his leading men. They had wearied of their dangerous and futile life on the run and had little desire to fight other Apache. They urged Geronimo to surrender. Knowing that the Mexicans would give him no quarter if captured, Geronimo met with General Crook and agreed to return north of the border. Yet the wily old leader could not quite bring himself to give up and fled once again with a handful of followers on March 29, 1886. His actions compromised Crook's position among his superiors in Washington, leading to his resignation. His replacement, General Nelson A. Miles, fully confident in the superiority of white soldiers over Indian "savages," took 5,000 U.S. troops, one-fourth of the regular army at the time, into the field to apprehend Geronimo's ragged band of 36 Apache. After months of fruitless campaigning, the footsore and weary troops had little to show for their efforts. Many Apache attributed Geronimo's success in eluding the troops to his powerfu relationship with coyote, the sly and canny hunter of the Southwestern deserts. In desperation, Miles finally turned to the Apache scouts.

Martine and Kayitah, two Chiricahua Apache scouts, agreed to accompany a white officer into Mexico and find Geronimo's camp. After a long search, the two scouts caught up with their kinsmen, something 5,000 American troops could never do. Years later, Eve Ball, a white woman collecting Apache oral testimonies, asked Martine's son George why his father had agreed to the dangerous mission. As recorded in the book *Apache Voices*, George remembered his father's words, "We got relatives up there [with Geronimo]," Martine said. "We want to take our people back so they won't suffer. . . . We tell Geronimo we came to help him and his people." Geronimo's followers agreed that a life on the run, separated from family and friends, led only to disappointment and certain death. The old leader concurred and on September 3,

1886, met with General Miles and formally surrendered. Soon he and his people boarded trains as prisoners of war to join their kin in exile.

The surrender of the Chiricahua Apache hastened the integration of the Southwest into the national economy. Railroad, mining, ranching, and agricultural corporations soon dominated the region. Paradoxically, the program of culture change relentlessly pushed at reservations gave the Apache little preparation for this new world. Everywhere they would face new challenges, as they sought to adapt to the "modern" world.

Cultural Persistence and Adaptation

Naiche, son of Cochise, picked up his paints and began to work. As he bent over the stretched hide, adding dabs of red or blue or yellow here and there, he cast his mind back to the cool mountain peaks of Arizona, dotted with pine trees and running with swift, cool streams. Yet the sweat dripping down his nose quickly brought his attention back to the present, to the hot and humid land called Florida, where his people lived in exile and imprisonment, amid sickness and disease.

More than ever they needed protection and healing, and so he painted the gahé, the powerful Mountain Spirits, dancing around the central fire, banishing all evil from the ritual space where a young woman became charged with the power of White Painted Woman, mother of all Apache. Next he added the family and female sponsors of the young woman to his painting. She relied on their guidance and wisdom. They helped her to follow the path laid down by Child of the Water and White Painted Woman in the far-off past of the people. As he painted, he remembered the story of how White Painted Woman gave the ceremony to the people, after her son had rid the world of monsters. Through its ritual, girls became women and contributed to the perpetuation of the people.

As the other Chiricahua Apache looked at Naiche's hide paintings—at the girl filled with the power of White Painted Woman, at the Mountain Spirits dancing around the central fire— they knew that as long as such powerful beings still lived among the Apache, they would survive, even the pain of captivity.

THE ATTACK ON IDENTITY

By the last quarter of the nineteenth century, all of the major Apache tribal groups found themselves on reservations or, as in the case of the Chiricahua, in exile, far from the Southwest. In the same way that relentless military campaigning had stripped away the Apache homelands, reservation agents now attempted to strip awayApache culture, mostly by trying to redefine traditional roles and behavior. Many reservation agents took their "civilizing mission" seriously, regarding Apache cultural practices as "primitive" and holding back progress. In 1895, for example, Lieutenant V. E. Stottler became the Mescalero Apache agent, launching an attack on Mescalero family structure in order to undermine the traditional role of elders, especially women, in setting tribal policy. As part of this campaign, he worked to stamp out mother-in-law avoidance, a traditional practice that reinforced a son-in-law's respect and support for his wife's mother and her family. He also prohibited all Apache ceremonies, especially the important puberty rituals that marked a young women's transition into adulthood.

Especially vulnerable to this program of radical cultural transformation were Apache children. "Indian reformers" convinced government policymakers that an educational program aimed at American Indian children had greater potential for success than one aimed at adults, whose behavior and beliefs were more deeply rooted and less susceptible to change. Moreover, they believed that removing children from their families and reservation settings, preferably to boarding schools established far in the East, would facilitate their education by minimizing "unwholesome" tribal influences. A willing Congress appropriated funds for Indian education, both for on- and off-reservation boarding schools, authorizing the commissioner of Indian affairs to do everything possible to enforce mandatory attendance, even to the point of withholding annuities and rations from stubborn parents. The ruling proved emotionally devastating to thousands of Indian parents.

To fill the boarding school established at the Mescalero Apache Reservation in 1884, for example, agent Fletcher J. Cowart resorted to force, regardless of the feelings of Apache parents. In a report to the commissioner of Indian affairs quoted by Morris Opler in his *Apache Odyssey*, he wrote:

> I found the attendance at boarding school about half what it should be, and at once set about increasing it to the full capacity of the accommodation. This I found extremely difficult. . . . Everything in the way of persuasion and argument having failed, it became necessary to visit the camps unexpectedly with a detachment of police, and seize such children as were proper and take them away to school, willing or unwilling. Some hurried their children off to the mountains or hid them away in camp, and the police had to chase and capture them like so many wild rabbits. This unusual proceeding created quite an outcry. The men were sullen and muttering, the women loud in their lamentations, and the children almost out of their wits with fright.

"I saw one girl caught by the police on horseback," a Mescalero informant told Opler. "You'd think her heart was going to break, the way she cried."

To one degree or another, all of the Apache groups faced a program of enforced cultural change at their respective reservations or in the boarding schools. Tirelessly, Apache worked to accommodate themselves to changing policies issued by individual agents, military personnel, or Washington bureaucrats, while attempting to preserve vital cultural values or adapt them to new circumstances. In essence, Apache people sought to preserve their identity in an ever-shifting world, sometimes in ways that adapted traditional beliefs to new roles and expectations, at other times by combining elements of the old and the new.

AT THE BOARDING SCHOOL

Despite their removal to the Pennsylvania-based Carlisle Indian Industrial Boarding School—an almost military-type school dedicated to eradicating all elements of Indian culture—Chiricahua children, for instance, found creative ways to maintain traditional Apache practices and values. Boys, in particular, found an outlet in sports. Traditional skills emphasizing strength and endurance could be honed through wrestling, football, or track and field events, which had the added attraction of allowing Apache boys to exchange their long pants for shorts, allowing the freedom of movement associated with a breechcloth. Perhaps because it combines strength, accuracy, and strategic thinking, football proved popular among the older boys, and the Carlisle players defeated a number of teams from eastern universities. Allowed to watch the contests, Apache girls cheered from their seats.

At Carlisle, Apache teenagers soon took on an almost parental role over their younger brothers, sisters, and cousins. They comforted them when sick, shared their food, and secretly kept their language alive, speaking in whispers in the dormitory sleeping quarters. Following accepted Apache practice, older children went out of their way to provide support and inspiration to the other children.

Notwithstanding their best efforts to maintain traditional Apache beliefs and modes of behavior, the Chiricahua children at Carlisle spent too much time at the school not to be unaffected by the experience. Some even became Christians. When they returned to their people, now relocated to Fort Sill, Oklahoma,

Many Apache were taken from reservations as children and sent to the Carlisle Indian Industrial Boarding School in Pennsylvania (*above*). By separating children from their parents and familiar surroundings, reformers hoped these young Native Americans would assimilate and become self-reliant, productive members of mainstream society.

their status as Carlisle graduates set them apart. At worst, this left some caught between two cultural worlds, never feeling fully at home in either one. At best, it gave some the skills necessary to navigate the white world, which constantly threatened to impinge upon and overwhelm the Apache people.

REFASHIONING ADULT ROLES
Increasingly unable to follow customary male pursuits of hunting, raiding, and warfare, Apache men adapted their traditional

roles to new circumstances as well. For a short while, service in the U.S. Army as scouts provided an approved outlet for their skills and energies. In many ways scouting resembled raiding. Men served with their male relatives, often in companies of 25 or so under the supervision of one or two white officers. Young Apache men also received the kind of guidance and mentorship that prepared them for adulthood. In fact, many Apache extended this mentorship to their white officers, young men new to the ways of war.

Alchesay
of the White Mountain Apache

The Apache have always respected individuals with particular skills and abilities. Some people excelled in hunting, others in medical knowledge, while others might know how to find mescal. Only a few, however, demonstrated the wide array of skills needed to lead people. Of these skills, probably the power of persuasion was greatest, as no chief had the power to force Apache along a particular course against their will.

Exercising leadership became increasingly difficult when reservation agents and military officials dominated decision making. Some Apache men became "tag-band" chiefs, appointed by the agents to help with such tasks as the distribution of rations. At the Fort Apache Reservation in Arizona, home to the White Mountain Apache band of the Western Apache, even this small amount of Apache leadership in reservation administration diminished by 1895. Agents appointed by the Bureau of Indian Affairs dispensed with the tag-band chief system and made all decisions of consequence, although sometimes they called together councils of leading men to inform them of decisions and to insist on their cooperation.

Nevertheless, among the White Mountain Apache, traditional leadership survived outside the official reservation

Sometimes these white officers received friendly teasing from the older, more experienced scouts. The young greenhorn lieutenant Britton Davis recalled how his scouts once good-naturedly offered him a roasted animal, not telling him it was a desert rat. Always hungry, the chubby Davis, whom the Apache nicknamed "Fat Boy," almost ate the tidbit but stopped himself as he saw the mirthful expressions on the scouts' faces. Davis joined in the laughter, unaware that the scouts probably considered him an apprentice warrior—still having to prove his worth on the trail.

system. In the early twentieth century Alchesay emerged as a strong voice for his people. Part of his authority stemmed from his experience as an Apache scout during the Chiricahua wars, winning a Medal of Honor and the respect of military officials like General George Crook. This provided him entry into the highest levels of the U.S. government, meeting with presidents Theodore Roosevelt and Warren G. Harding to advocate for his people. As a result, even reservation agents tended to include him when informing leading men of new policies and procedures. Among his own people, however, much of his authority stemmed from his knowledge of the white world, and his realization that the Apache would have to adapt in order to navigate this strange new world.

Alchesay became a tireless advocate of education, urging young Apache to learn how to read and write English and to gain the skills that would allow them to compete among whites. He encouraged Apache parents to take advantage of the free education offered their children, to endure the separation that inevitably occurred, all to ensure a future generation of leaders among the White Mountain Apache. When Congress finally passed the Indian Reorganization Act in 1934 restoring tribal government, White Mountain Apache leaders were ready to come to the fore, following a path laid down by Chief Alchesay.

With the end of the "Apache wars" diminishing scouting opportunities, other Apache men carved out familiar roles in the new world of wage work. Now instead of leaving home to hunt or raid, Apache men traveled to off-reservation work sites for weeks or months, working in the booming railroad, agriculture, and mining trades. At the San Carlos Reservation, for example, Apache men built the first rail lines through the reservation, linking such towns as Globe, Safford, and Bowie. In the meantime, women remained at home, maintaining the family unit. This reinforced the pattern of matrilocal residence, in which a young married man lived with his wife and her family, and matrilineal descent, in which Apache traced kinship through the female line.

On reservations that contained good grazing land, some Apache became cowboys, caring for and raising livestock as once they had raised horses. At the Fort Apache Reservation, for instance, agent C.W. Crouse encouraged ranching to lessen Apache dependence on government rations. He established a small herd and even designed the first brand—a broken arrow to symbolize the transition from war to peace and the letters "ID," standing for "Indian Department." From these beginnings, individual Apache families began to take up ranching in earnest. Among these ranchers, Wallace Altaha, known more familiarly by his identification tag number R-14, prospered in supplying cattle to the military. Working with his extended family—two brothers-in-law, a sister, and a brother—he eventually built up a herd of 10,000 head of cattle.

In Oklahoma, ranching played an indirect role in supporting Kiowa-Apache families. When the government broke up some tribal land holdings under the General Allotment Act of 1887 and assigned small homesteads to individual Apache and their families, many Kiowa-Apache refused to live on their land, preferring instead to live among their relatives in two small communities, away from larger white towns. They earned income from their land by leasing it out for grazing to white ranchers. Many Kiowa-Apache spent their money on traveling to peyote meetings of the

One way Apache were able to leave the reservation was to serve as scouts for the U.S. Army. Scouting allowed Apache men to use the skills they had learned from their elders.

Native American Church held all across the state. In this way they maintained their ties with the Comanche and the Kiowa, while preserving, to a degree, the nomadic lifestyle of pre-reservation, pre-Allotment days, much to the annoyance of federal officials.

RELIGIOUS ACCOMMODATION

Traditional Apache religious belief had long provided the people with a means of understanding and coping with an uncertain world. During the reservation years, Apache struggled to maintain their religious practices and beliefs, even as reservation personnel sought to undermine or redirect religious ceremonies, while actively promoting Christianity. Sometimes this led to strategic changes in religious practice. Many Fort Sill Apache (Chiricahua) had joined the Dutch Reformed Church, a Protestant denomination active in mission work among American Indians. Nevertheless, they clung to their reverence for the Mountain Spirits, even on the plains of Oklahoma, and continued to hold ritual dances. At the same time, however, tribal leaders decided to retire the puberty rite for young women. They realized that few families had the resources to commit to the four-day ritual. Moreover, away from the mountains of their ancestors, they could not obtain such necessary items as lodge poles with which to construct the young woman's special shelter needed during the ceremony.

Also in the east, Lipan Apache were instrumental in the spread of the peyote religion, the basis for the Native American Church, more formally organized by Chief Quanah Parker of the Comanche and other Plains Indian leaders in the 1890s. For generations Indian peoples in Mexico had harvested small beans or "buttons" from the fleshy part of the peyote cactus. When ingested—through chewing or brewed into a tea and drunk— peyote heightened spiritual consciousness and promoted healing. Remnants of the Lipan Apache who sought refuge among the Mescalero introduced the ritual. Later, at the urging of Parker, they brought it to Oklahoma. Parker himself then began to introduce peyote use to his people as an alternative to Christianity. Under great pressure to shed their tribal identity by white missionaries and government officials in the process of allotting Comanche tribal lands, the peyote religion, formalized as the Native American Church, served as a vital unifying force among the Comanche, Kiowa, Kiowa-Apache, and other peoples, reinforcing community and tribal values over the individualism preached by whites.

Some Apache incorporated Christian elements into traditional religious practices. Among the Western Apache, who by the 1920s had received attention at various times from Lutheran, Catholic, Mormon, and Assembly of God missionaries, strong medicine men became the center of movements that promised people a better world, away from the difficult adjustments demanded by the reservation. These religious leaders often urged their followers to reform their lives in preparation for the coming of this new world.

Neil Buck described to the ethnologist Grenville Goodwin how he was introduced to the teachings of the medicine man Daslahdn at Cibecue, a small community on the Fort Apache Reservation. "I was about twenty-three years old and out of school when the [movement] started," Buck remembered. "It was meant to be raised up on top of a cloud like Jesus was. I can remember it well. The first we heard of it was from Cibecue. A man called Daslahdn, a medicine-man, started it in 1903. He said he was going to raise the people up." In his ceremony, Daslahdn used stories and songs familiar to the people from the girls' puberty rite, as well as songs given to him by the Lightning People, from whom he had received his power. Other shamans involved in the movement used sweat baths and other traditional practices. By 1907, however, the movement largely died out, as the ascension into the clouds and the coming of a new world of plenty and peace failed to occur.

Silas John Edwards, a medicine man born at Fort Apache, started the so-called "Holy Grounds" movement in 1921, again incorporating Apache and Christian symbols and practices. Following a vision in which he climbed a rainbow to receive religious instruction from Ussen, or "Giver of Life," Silas John began to preach a return to the old ways as a means to attain salvation, even traveling as far as the Mescalero Reservation to spread his message. His words fell on fertile ground, especially among that generation of Apache who felt lost between the traditional life and culture and the strange, frightening world of the whites. Ruth McDonald Boyer and Narcissus Duffy Gayton captured one of these voices in their book *Apache Mothers and Daughters*. Bashád-e, a granddaughter of Victorio, characterized her world of the 1920s in mournful terms:

> With all the terrible things that have happened to us since I was a young girl—even here in Mescalero, the Anglos had done nothing but betray us, tell us one thing and do another—well, I just know there must be something more. I don't know what. I do know my grandchildren must learn to cope with white ways, but it is just too much to ask of me. Somehow my mother, Dilth-cleyhen, seems resigned—more than I am. She clings to our old customs and ignores everything new. But I am tired. I can't learn English at my age. I can't read or write. I don't know when they are cheating me. Maybe this Silas has the answers.

Like Bashád-e, some Apache expressed feelings of fear, frustration, and bewilderment as they contemplated the vast changes that had occurred in Apache life in as little as two generations. And indeed, from one vantage, there was much to be pessimistic about. Federal policies designed to create prosperous and integrated Native Americans had instead led to poverty and reduced opportunities. Reservations still suffered higher rates of tuberculosis, pneumonia, and other diseases. Education was of the most basic sort and often out of step with the modern industrial world. Yet from another vantage, the Apache could be seen drawing on their deep wellsprings of strength to preserve an Apache identity in a changing world.

New Ways Open

The United States senator had read the Meriam Report, but he and his colleagues had to see things for themselves. Traveling by train and car over endless miles of prairie and desert, they visited reservation after reservation, interviewing everyone about the "state" of American Indians. Finally in 1931, they came to Mescalero. Approaching out of the flat, hot desert, they gradually made their way into the Sacramento Mountains, marveling at the 12,000-foot-high (3,650-meter-high) peak, Sierra Blanca, its crown still snow-covered. The air was crisp and cool, with fine stands of pine.

Surely there could be no poverty here, the senator thought. Not with all this bounty. At the hearing later that day, however, Solon Sombrero from the little reservation town of Elk Springs told the senator that the people were always in debt. The tribe owed for road construction, for the upkeep of its herd, and, of course, for goods bought on credit at the agency store. What about the timber, the senator inquired. That goes to the support of the agency, Sombrero revealed. As the questioning continued, the senator finally began to understand. Most of the tribal income from timber, cattle or sheep, and the like went to the U.S. Treasury. From there it was appropriated to the reservation agency to run its operations and pay for special projects like road construction. Twice a year, small disbursements of funds came to individual Mescalero from these assets, but for the rest of the year, they had to use credit to purchase necessities. In essence, they were working twice to earn back their own money: the first time when their timber or grazing income was sent to Washington, the second time when the money came back to fund the agent's special projects.

And the projects had done nothing for Mescalero families. The people were hungry and needed better housing, but by the logic of the reservation, the agent and the government knew what was best, not the people. The senator and his staff listened. Maybe Meriam had been right after all. Something would have to change, not only for the Mescalero Apache, but also for Native peoples all over the United States.

THE "INDIAN NEW DEAL"

For many Americans, the 1930s were the decade of the economic disaster known as the Great Depression. In its opening years, hungry men and women lined the streets in major American cities to receive food. Thousands of families lost their homes. Most tellingly, 11 million people (25 percent of the labor force) could not find work. Yet, for these same Americans, the 1930s were also the decade of the New Deal, President Franklin D. Roosevelt's plan of relief, recovery, and reform, in one way or another touching most Americans, assuring them that the federal government was working on their behalf to create jobs and ensure security.

In one sense, the onset of the Great Depression among American Indians simply marked a continuation of poverty and limited opportunity. As Lewis Meriam's 1928 study *The Problem of Indian Administration*, sometimes called the Meriam Report, had revealed, their "great depression" had begun years earlier with reservation and Allotment policies that curtailed tribal independence and opportunity. Nevertheless, Native America would experience an "Indian New Deal," a similar program of reform and recovery. This Indian New Deal encompassed a number of reforms, including an end to Allotment and the restoration of "surplus" tribal lands. Arguably its greatest innovation lay, however, in reconstituting tribal governments. Although the federal government's preferred type of tribal government—constitutionally based and democratic—derived from Anglo-European models, it nevertheless opened a space for a reassertion of American Indian self-government and leadership

APACHE TRIBAL COUNCILS

Launched in the midst of the Great Depression and the New Deal, Apache tribal councils focused much of their attention on economic issues. How could reservation resources be developed to benefit the tribe? Were there jobs and opportunities available to tribal members? Did tribal members have adequate housing and access to services?

One of the most energetic of the new tribal councils was found at the Mescalero Reservation. Mescalero delegates had traveled to Santo Domingo Pueblo in 1934 to learn about the Indian Reorganization Act (IRA) and its provisions. They returned to Mescalero determined to take advantage of the opportunity for greater self-government provided under the act. In 1936 the reservation adopted a constitution and established a Business Committee to operate as a new tribal government. Prominently, the new constitution recognized as tribal members all people enrolled on the 1935 census of the tribe, an action that meant that no distinction would be made between the Mescalero and the relocated Chiricahua and Lipan Apache who had come to the reservation before that time. Accordingly, Asa Daklugie, son of Chief Juh of the Chiricahua of Mexico, served as president of the Business Committee in 1938, as did Chiricahua Sam Kenoi in 1939 and 1940. Like Daklugie, Kenoi had attended the Carlisle Indian Industrial School.

The Mescalero Business Committee set out to develop reservation resources to benefit the tribe. Through the Mescalero Cattle Growers Association, for example, the committee members reasserted control over grazing lands, which had been leased to non-Apache ranchers by previous reservation agents, and turned them over to tribal members. They exercised new borrowing powers to seek federal funds to build homes and farms, as well as develop a lumber industry for the largely mountainous and forested reservation. New reservation agents or superintendents generally supported these endeavors, especially the move to build new permanent housing on the reservation, a challenge given the Apache practice of abandoning homes after a death. Nevertheless, by 1942 each reservation family had a new house, generally four-roomed with a galvanized iron roof.

Like the Mescalero, the Jicarilla Apache organized a new formal government, adopting a constitution and bylaws in 1937. To direct tribal economic growth and protect tribal resources, they also adopted a corporate charter, establishing an entity similar to the Mescalero Business Committee. One of their first actions was to purchase the old reservation trading post where many tribal members came to buy necessities and other goods. Renamed the Jicarilla Apache Cooperative, the trading post now operated as a nonprofit entity, a signal of its new role serving tribal interests. In the same way, the council dealt with the issue of allotments, organizing new regulations under which to use land, putting the principle of tribal benefit over individual gain.

The White Mountain Apache also formed a constitutionally based government, organizing a Tribal Council in 1938. Yet the deference given to traditional headmen such as Chief Alchesay

In the 1930s, several Apache groups were able to regain control of their lands from the federal government and establish a governing Tribal Council. Above, the Indian Agency on the Jicarilla Apache Reservation in 1938.

continued, in this case through his successor, Chief Baha. Chief Baha and other elders realized that the educational skills of the younger generation could be put to good use through service on the Tribal Council. There, they could help to negotiate with non-Apache like Bureau of Indian Affairs personnel and other federal and state officials, as well as neighboring non-Apache communities, in order to accomplish long-range development of reservation resources. Traditional leaders especially played a major role in convincing other Apache that development projects that seemed to fall outside of Apache cultural norms still could be pursued and, in fact, provide real benefits. Fish, for example, were never a major part of traditional subsistence and were often associated with snakes and other "evil" animals, but were avidly sought by non-Apache anglers, especially in the swift mountain streams of the White Mountain Reservation. Why not open the reservation to non-Apache fishermen, capturing income in the form of licensing fees? As Chief Baha pointed out to reluctant Apache, when they worked in nearby white communities like Globe or Holbrook, Arizona, they paid to stay in hotels, purchase meals, and even park their cars, feeding coins into parking meters. Non-Apache could do the same, paying for their access to, in this case, reservation recreational opportunities.

Not all Apache, however, chose to participate in the Indian New Deal. Those Chiricahua now called the Fort Sill Apache declined to organize a government under the provisions of the Oklahoma Indian Welfare Act of 1936, which extended IRA opportunities to the tribes of Oklahoma. Their history as prisoners of war made them suspicious of new government initiatives. Moreover, many had forged individual identities as farmers, ranchers, or soldiers and feared being thrust back into the role of "Reservation Indians." Although many took advantage of more general New Deal programs such as the Civilian Conservation Corps or the Works Progress Administration, federal programs designed to provide jobs during the lean Depression years, they held aloof from initiatives aimed explicitly at American Indian peoples.

Even though not all Apache participated in the opportunities presented by the Indian New Deal, the New Deal era as a whole began to break down reservation isolation. Tribal governments intent on developing resources played a role in this, as did the federal government, whose many and varied economic initiatives provided off-reservation work for many Apache. Accelerating this process, however, was an event that occurred thousands of miles away from Apache country: the Japanese attack on American naval forces at Pearl Harbor, Hawaii.

WORLD WAR II

The Japanese attack on American forces at Pearl Harbor in December 1941 brought the United States into World War II, which had been raging since 1939. Across the nation, American Indians rushed to enlist. By 1942, 99 percent of eligible American Indians had registered for the draft, the highest number among all ethnic groups nationwide. By war's end, more than 44,500 American Indian men and women had served in the armed forces. Patriotism, the desire to defend their country from harm, motivated most of these young men and women. Beyond this, however, many also enlisted to defend their homelands, the sacred sites their people had occupied since time immemorial. In defending the United States, they were protecting a land whose every stream and stone carried a story of family and kin and people.

Many American Indians also had a long tradition of serving in the American military, from the Revolutionary War down through World War I. In fact, 12,000 American Indians, 85 percent of them volunteers, served in World War I, paving the way for American citizenship for all Indian peoples with the Indian Citizenship Act of 1924. Apache reflected this tradition, serving as scouts during the Apache wars of the 1870s and 1880s and continuing their service into the twentieth century through such events as the 1916 Pershing expedition into Mexico to apprehend Francisco "Pancho" Villa.

Accordingly, without waiting for the draft, fully one-fourth of the Mescalero Apache tribe enlisted in the military, led by Tribal Council president Homer Yahanoza, soon dispatched to the Philippines. So high were the enlistments that in 1942 the tribe could muster only 25 herd riders out of their usual 50 to drive 8,000 livestock, valued at $75,000, to market. The Apache not only contributed to the war effort as soldiers, but also, like many other Americans, as workers in the growing defense-related industries.

This huge demand for labor triggered a vast migration among all American people to the industrial cities of the Northeast and Midwest as well as both coasts. Apache, like other American Indians, followed the trend, moving to such cities as Los Angeles for high-paying defense jobs. And the defense industry, building the ships, tanks, trucks, and planes needed for the war effort, had a voracious appetite for resources. Again, tribal governments stepped to the fore, diverting reservation resources to the war

Allan Houser

World-renowned Chiricahua Apache artist and sculptor Allan Houser (1914–1994) received one of his first major sculpture commissions from the Alumni Association of the Haskell Institute in Lawrence, Kansas. Although little trained in sculpture at the time, Houser entered the design competition for a war memorial to honor the school's American Indian World War II soldiers.

The first Chiricahua Apache born after the tribe's release from captivity in 1913, Houser was a member of the Warm Springs or eastern band of Chiricahua. His father and mother elected to stay at Fort Sill when the Chiricahua were given the choice of moving to Mescalero, New Mexico, or remaining in Oklahoma. Houser's parents raised him in the tradition of the Dutch Reformed Church, a Protestant denomination that had carried out mission work among the Chiricahua, and in the traditional ways of the Apache. At age 20, after some years at both boarding schools and public school, he decided to develop his interest in painting. As recorded in W. Jackson Rushing III's study of his art, Houser declared, "I had learned a great deal about tribal customs from my father and my mother, and the more I learned the more I wanted to effort. Working through the War Resources Council of the federal government, the Fort Apache Reservation, for instance, supplied timber to the military building boom set in motion by the war.

Among boarding school students and alumni, enlistments also ran high. Schools brought together Indian peoples from many tribes and fostered a sense of common dedication and purpose. Students and alumni of such institutions as Haskell Institute in Lawrence, Kansas, or the Santa Fe Indian School in Santa Fe, New Mexico,

put it down on canvas or something. That's pretty much how I started."

In 1934 Houser relocated to the Santa Fe Indian School to study art. Although the school, like Carlisle Indian Industrial School, operated along strict, almost military-like lines and offered mainly vocational training programs, its art teacher, Dorothy Dunn, believed that American Indian art had much to offer world culture. Her classes in "authentic" American Indian art, reflecting techniques, subjects, and themes before contact with non-Natives, however, did not always sit well with Houser. He wished to study such topics as anatomy and life drawing to inform his own style, which incorporated both traditional and contemporary approaches. His decision to enter the Haskell design competition reflected his interest in contemporary American Indian life, such as participation in World War II.

After winning the design competition, he set out to turn a huge block of marble into a sculptural piece. Not even owning the "proper" tools, he used a jackhammer and any other tools he could borrow or adapt to his purposes to create a seven-foot-high (2.1-meter-high) monumental figure. Upright, grave, wrapped in a blanket, this *Comrade in Mourning* stands above a war bonnet and lance, silently remembering the many American Indians who gave their lives for their country in World War II.

Celebrated sculptor Allan Houser is one of the most famous Apache in the world. His work, which includes the Native American World War II memorial *Comrade in Mourning* in Lawrence, Kansas, combines modern art forms with traditional images.

enlisted in the military and served with distinction throughout the war. In many ways, these soldiers supported each other, drawing strength from a common identity as Native Americans, even though individuals might represent different tribes and cultural traditions. Fostering these ties as well were organizations like the Santa Fe Indian Club, which provided social networking opportunities for servicemen and servicewomen and, perhaps most importantly, published a newsletter that let Indian families—mainly Pueblo, Hopi, Navajo, and Mescalero and White Mountain Apache—read about their loved ones far from home.

In her study of the American Indian contributions to World War II, historian Jeré Bishop Franco mined these newsletters to uncover something of the everyday lives of servicemen and servicewomen abroad, especially Mescalero and White Mountain Apache. Mescalero Apache Private Alfred Kayitah, for instance, who helped to liberate Italy during the war, wrote of the "most wonderful experience in all my life. I got to see the city of Rome." He went on to marvel at the sights and sounds of Rome, including St. Peter's Basilica, where he heard the pope speak. Others, like Seaman William Ethelbah, wrote of the joy of receiving packages from home, good-humoredly adding that their temporary windfall made them quite popular among their comrades: "You can't imagine what a package from home means to one here. I was pretty popular til they emptied the box and that didn't take very long." Sometimes these young servicemen used the newsletter to seek out tribal friends, writing in their queries concerning a friend or relative's location with the hope that they would read it and respond. Transferred to Italy, Justin Herrera, for instance, hoped to find Alfred Kayitah, a familiar face from home among the many thousands of new faces and new experiences set in motion by the war.

For these young Apache men and women, like their counterparts in mainstream America, the war provided a wealth of opportunities. For the first time many interacted with people outside their culture—white Americans, Europeans, and Asians—broadening their concept of the world. They also acquired new skills and adapted old ones to novel circumstances. They received recognition for their services, many returning home with medals and other commendations. Unlike mainstream America, however, the war also caused them to reflect upon their position in American society. Many still encountered discrimination and prejudice in the white world. On the reservation, the Bureau of Indian Affairs still played too large a role in regulating tribal life and resources. For these young men and women, the battle for freedom continued.

Apache Rebirth

The Fort Sill Apache woman and her family had been Christians for years, members of the Apache Reformed Church, an off-shoot of the Dutch Reformed Church. Yet, she pointed out to the interviewer, her Apache and Christian beliefs ran side by side. Fire, for one, played a great role in Apache religion, for around the sacred fire danced the mighty Mountain Spirits bringing protection and healing. Likewise, the Holy Spirit had appeared in tongues of fire to the apostles, who brought the good news and healing to all people. Similarly, Moses had gone up into the mountains to speak with the Lord, and did not the Apache venerate the mountains as sacred places?

In the Bible, the evangelist Matthew reminded all people to be like the birds of the air, neither sowing nor reaping nor storing away food in barns. And like the birds, the old woman said, we Apache live for today, depending on each other and sharing with each other. That is the Indian way. The interviewer nodded in understanding. There were so many things, the woman continued, about our people that I hope we never lose.

By the mid-twentieth century, generations of Apache had attended white-run schools, had listened to Protestant and Catholic missionaries, and had lived and worked away from their reservation homes. Yet many continued to cherish their Apache heritage and culture, while embracing new experiences and roles. Non-Apache sometimes failed to appreciate this duality, creating new challenges for the Apache people.

Surveying the thousands of American Indians who honorably served in World War II as soldiers or workers, the United States government, for example, wrongly concluded that assimilation—the merging of Indian peoples into the white mainstream—was the wave of the future. Policymakers back in Washington believed that the trends set in motion by the war—particularly the migration of American Indian peoples to urban areas for defense work—would provide a basis for a directed, sponsored relocation policy after the war. As more and more American Indians entered the off-reservation workforce, policymakers reasoned, additional federal services to reservations could be decreased, until agencies like the Bureau of Indian Affairs would no longer need to exist.

Perhaps policymakers mistook American Indian defense of the country—the coming together of all Americans to defeat the Axis powers and restore freedom and democracy to the world—as a rejection of tribal and cultural identity. On the contrary, American Indians served their country both as American citizens and tribal citizens—as proud Iroquois, Cherokee, Navajo, or Apache nations, cherishing the ties of family and homeland within the larger American fabric. Policymakers seemed to forget that a nation like the Apache, who for centuries had interacted with Spaniards, Mexicans, and Americans, had never forgotten who they were as a people. At peace establishment, reservation, boarding school, or exile, they were always Apache.

THE "REBIRTH" OF THE FORT SILL APACHE

In the post–World War II world, probably the Fort Sill Apache best demonstrate the extraordinary strength of tribal identity. To the casual observer, the Fort Sill Apache seemed the least "Apache." Descendants of the Chiricahua who had elected to remain in Oklahoma, as opposed to the majority of the tribe that relocated to the Mescalero Reservation, were now considered "small town" Americans, living in rural isolation on scattered allotments. They were sometimes farmers or ranchers, little different from their non-Apache neighbors eking out a similar hardscrabble life. Their rejection of tribal organization in the Indian New Deal era seemingly confirmed this view, as they stubbornly refused to "return to the reservation." Similarly, the emphasis on education shown by many Fort Sill Apache families, whose children attended boarding schools in the East or throughout Oklahoma and the Southwest, often led many young Apache to seek employment out of state, a trend that continued in the 1950s as many quit farming, unable to afford the growing investments of machinery and fertilizers needed to make agriculture profitable. In other developments, fluency in the Apache language had declined, and membership in the Apache Reformed Church had increased. Indeed, by 1958, the Bureau of Indian Affairs had targeted the Fort Sill Apache, along with other Indian tribes, for official "Termination," an end to the federal-tribal relationship and a termination of federal oversight and services.

Yet, below the notice of the Bureau of Indian Affairs, Apache cultural traits and values continued unabated. Elders still told their children and grandchildren stories of the old days and sang traditional tribal songs. Healing knowledge remained, especially in the hands of skilled practitioners like Sam Haozous, the father of Allan Houser, who used local herbs to brew medicinal teas. Indeed, many a boarding school student swore by his eye drops, said to cure trachoma. Most tellingly, the Fort Sill people, in exile far from their mountain homes in Arizona, continued to hold in

Apache living on the Mesaclero Reservation (*above*) have more opportunities to learn customs and rituals than those living far away from their ancestral lands. Communities in Fort Sill, Oklahoma, and throughout the country maintain the Apache traditions through storytelling, singing, and healing.

reverence the powerful Mountain Spirits, great beings of healing, blessing, and protection, commemorated and honored in dance.

Providing even more cultural glue, the long historical memory of the Fort Sill Apache bound the people together: their betrayal by an American government that sent the Chiricahua Apache scouts into exile after years of faithful service in the military; their long ordeal as prisoners of war; the loss of their tribal homelands in Arizona and New Mexico as well as the loss of their homes at Fort Sill during Allotment—all these the people remembered, nursing in their hearts a desire for justice. From their time in Oklahoma, the people had organized informal tribal committees to press their claims, although it was not until 1946 that the passage of the Indian Claims Commission Act provided an avenue for success.

Passed by a Congress wishing to divest the American government of responsibility for American Indian peoples, the Indian Claims Commission Act was designed to settle all outstanding claims that tribes held against the United States—claims for land loss, mismanagement of tribal funds and assets, failed treaty obligations, and the like. Tribes whose claims were recognized by an Indian Claims Court would be monetarily compensated for their losses. The Fort Sill Apache lost no time in pressing their case, seeking redress for the "unlawful" removal of the people from their homelands and their "unlawful" arrest and imprisonment.

The Fort Sill Apache, however, found the claims process far from smooth. At one point, for example, the court refused to take up the issue of the tribe's unlawful imprisonment, arguing that it fell outside its jurisdiction. At other times, it ruled that the tribe itself was but a "collection of individuals," as it had not reorganized itself in the 1930s. Even a seemingly straightforward question such as the amount of land formerly held by the Apache in Arizona and New Mexico led to years of wrangling. Finally in 1973 all outstanding issues were resolved, and the tribe received more than $16 million in compensation. More importantly, however, the process encouraged the people to organize an official tribal government under a BIA-recognized constitution. Launched in 1976, the new Fort Sill Apache Tribe of Oklahoma elected its first slate of officers, including chairperson Mildred Imoch Cleghorn, born a prisoner of war in 1910. Cleghorn and the new council made cultural and community cohesion a centerpiece of their new administration. For other Apache tribes,

economic and social welfare issues dominated the years following World War II.

MESCALERO AND WESTERN APACHE RESERVATION DEVELOPMENT

After World War II, the population of the Mescalero Apache
Reservation grew to 876 people, particularly as veterans returned
from the war and began to start families. A number of these
Apache took up government offers of relocation assistance and
moved to Los Angeles and San Francisco to seek employment.
However, in a trend reflected nationwide by many American
Indian families, most of these Apache soon returned to New
Mexico, as the transition from a largely rural reservation made
up of small towns to large urban metropolises often proceeded
less than smoothly. Added to the accelerated pace and demands of
urban living—navigating unfamiliar transportation systems, finding work, finding living quarters, and the like—Apache families
suffered from homesickness: the pull of the mountains, family,
and friends. Returning to the reservation, they threw themselves
into tribal plans for reservation development.

The development of reservation resources to provide jobs and
a higher standard of living, however, necessitated access to capital,
that is, money to invest in development projects. The tribe found
some of this money through an awards settlement from the Indian
Claims Court. In 1967 the tribe received $8.5 million in compen-
sation, 80 percent of which it invested. Drawing on this and other
sources, the tribe under chair Wendell Chino, who would dominate Mescalero politics for the next several decades, concentrated
on promoting the tourism and recreation potential of the forested
reservation.

By this time the winds from Washington had shifted again.
While the Bureau of Indian Affairs and Congress had earlier
encouraged relocation of American Indians to urban areas
and the termination of the tribal-federal relationship, later

Mildred Imoch Cleghorn

In 1997, Mildred Imoch Cleghorn, age 87, tragically died in an automobile accident. Two years before, she had retired from her position as chair of the Fort Sill Apache Tribe, a position she had held for almost 20 years. She and others had led the fight to formally organize the tribe and to preserve Apache culture and history.

Mildred Cleghorn was the first chairperson elected to the Fort Sill tribal government.

Born into captivity in 1910, Cleghorn embodied the spirit of her grandfather, who had fought with Geronimo. Like many Apache children of her generation, she attended boarding school. And like many women of her generation, when she attended college, she received a degree in home economics, a course of study designed to give young women skills in home management. She spent the early part of her career in Kansas, Oklahoma, and New Mexico as a

administrations became more involved with their federal obligations, often outlined in treaties, toward American Indians. Many of these obligations, particularly as they dealt with the health, education, and well-being of American Indians, paralleled government support for the well-being of all Americans. The Great Society programs of President Lyndon Johnson, for example, opened new sources of federal funding to tribes, as well as cities and states more generally, and provided greater social and educational services. Drawing on such resources, the home extension agent, working among rural women to foster their household management knowledge and skills. Later she taught home economics at a number of public schools and became active in the Apache Reformed Church.

Like other Fort Sill Apache, Cleghorn worked to maintain Apache culture and values, even as government educational and Allotment policies made this a constant struggle. She especially excelled in beadwork and doll making, creating reproductions of Chiricahua and Warm Springs Apache and their traditional dress (her work would later be exhibited at the Smithsonian Institution in Washington, D.C.). Her crucial role in the long battle to achieve tribal recognition and compensation for past injustices, a battle only won in the 1970s, led to Cleghorn's election as tribal leader in 1976. During her time in office, she worked with the Tribal Council to expand economic opportunities, particularly the development of tribal enterprises that would provide jobs for Apache who had left the reservation to seek employment elsewhere. To further these efforts, she cultivated relations with other Oklahoma tribes, which were facing many of the same issues. During her long career, Cleghorn inspired generations of Fort Sill Apache to rediscover their tribal heritage and culture.

Mescalero established a Head Start program on the reservation. An early childhood intervention program, Head Start provided an educational boost to young children and their families, a benefit that translated to a smoother transition into elementary school. Likewise, a Job Corps center opened on the reservation to provide education and vocational training to young adults. As the tribe established tribal enterprises such as a ski resort, a fish hatchery, and a forestry industry, a growing core of trained Apache were ready to step into supervisory positions.

Native American leaders like Wendell Chino (*above*) use the Tribal Council to boost the economy and encourage conservation on the reservation. Chino, one of the most successful Apache leaders in recent history, was president of the Mescalero Apache for 34 years.

In 1975 Congress passed the Indian Self-Determination and Education Assistance Act, striking a blow against the paternalistic policies of the past. The act gave tribal governments, rather than federal officials, the right and the means to administer their own education and social assistance programs, as well as increased the involvement of Indian parents in educational decisions, particularly through school boards. In other words, this legislation recognized that tribes, like states, had a direct interest in working with the federal government to enhance the educational, social, and economic welfare of their citizens. The Mescalero, like other American Indian tribes, soon took over many of the functions and services long administered by the Bureau of Indian Affairs.

Western Apache groups on reservations in Arizona also took up the challenge of increased social and economic development. The White Mountain Apache of the Fort Apache Reservation, for instance, like the Mescalero, focused on the recreational potential of the reservation to non-Apache. In 1954 the Tribal Council created the White Mountain Recreation Enterprise to increase tribal income through the development and promotion of fishing, hunting, camping, and other tourist activities. To enhance fishing opportunities, the tribe also created artificial lakes and ponds to be stocked with game fish.

All of this activity took some non-Apache Arizonans by surprise, particularly those who had diverted reservation resources to other uses over the years with little interference from the Bureau of Indian Affairs and reservation agents. The Salt River Valley Water Users Association, for one, took legal action to prevent the damming of the Salt River, whose source lay on reservation land. At issue here was the preemption of water resources in the arid Southwest by growing desert cities like Phoenix, reaching out to acquire water rights in all directions, often hundreds of miles from the city. The association obtained an injunction, or court order, against the construction of a dam on the reservation. The Tribal Council under Chair Lester Oliver and Vice Chair Nelson Lupe immediately took action.

In a dramatic turn of events, the tribe blocked all access to the dam construction site with bulldozers and stationed armed guards around the work site. They stopped state law enforcement officials trying to enter the work site, informing them that only tribal police or U.S. marshals, as agents of the federal government, could enter the reservation to enforce the court order. In the meantime, construction crews worked nonstop to finish the dam, completing the job in 10 days. Although legal proceedings dragged on for another decade, in 1966 a federal judge dismissed the action, basically siding with the tribe. The purposeful action of the White Mountain Apache reminded Arizonans that federally recognized tribes, like states, exercised broad powers of self-government and control in their territories, a concept known as sovereignty.

In the same spirit, individual Apache families everywhere worked to enhance their children's future, particularly through education, as they realized that effective self-government and independence demanded the development of specialized skills. Narcissus Duffy Gayton, for example, a registered nurse and a leader in the development of health care on the Mescalero Reservation, voiced the concerns of many Apache when she told her nieces to aim their sights high. When she learned that her nieces wanted to attend an off-reservation school to acquire secretarial skills, she exclaimed, "That is not enough. You must study further and become specialized. Then you will be respected. Your services will be in demand." To her own daughter she gave similar advice: "You must study hard. You must go to college. A college education is something no one can take from you. I want you to be independent enough that you can stand up and look the next person right in the eye. You need not be abusive about it, but you are an Apache and you should be proud."

Self-government and Sovereignty in Apache Country Since 1990

Rufina tossed and turned. She could not sleep. She kept thinking about something her mother had mentioned. The Tribal Council had begun to talk about taking on a new enterprise, one guaranteed to bring millions of dollars a year to the reservation. Certainly the Tribal Council had fostered many economic development projects over the years under Wendell Chino's leadership. Hadn't he once joked that the Navajo make rugs, the Pueblo Indians make pottery, but the Mescalero make money? It seemed that way. Sixteen million board feet of lumber poured from the tribal sawmill every year. Seven thousand cattle grazed on tribal land. A quarter of a million people came each year to enjoy the slopes of Ski Apache, many staying at the Inn of the Mountain Gods, with its golf course, casino, and private lake. These enterprises had created hundreds of jobs for the Mescalero. But there were always additional needs—money to provide college scholarships, to provide the latest and best in medical care, to build good roads, to create highly skilled, good-paying jobs to keep the young people at home. "Ghost bullets," Chino told the elders, ghost bullets will bring the tribe new resources for the future.

And what were ghost bullets? They were the white man's nuclear waste. Over the years nuclear power plants had generated hundreds of tons of waste. Where would it be put? The federal government planned to store it in Nevada, deep under Yucca Mountain. But until that site could be prepared, it needed a temporary storage place—a place easily reached but not heavily populated, a place like, say, the Mescalero Reservation. In the same way the reservation had once leased land to white ranchers for grazing, it could now lease land for storing nuclear wastes, leases that could bring in tens of millions of dollars a year. The council trusted that the people would approve.

Inside and outside of the reservation, people were uneasy. Nuclear waste storage! Was it safe? What if radioactivity leaked out and got into the air or water. What would that do to people's health? What would it do to the tourist trade in Ruidoso, asked the white proprietors of restaurants and shops? What would it do to the reputation of New Mexico, wondered the governor in Santa Fe? Surely the negatives outweighed the positives. Yet Wendell Chino told them all that this was an Apache decision, not one for the white man or the white man's government in Santa Fe.

Her head filled with these troubled thoughts, Rufina finally slept. A strange dream troubled her slumber, however, and she awoke the next morning, unrested and disturbed. For a week she brooded on her dream, every night trying to figure out its meaning. And then one morning she awoke and understood. She would oppose the council's plan. She would persuade the people of its dangers.

As the twentieth century drew to a close, tribal governments continued to grapple with myriad issues, including managing natural resources, developing economic opportunities, providing social services, educating young people, preserving traditions and sacred sites, and protecting the environment. Many times they had to fight with Washington to receive attention to American Indian needs. In the press of national issues, Congress constantly under-funded appropriations for the Indian Health Service, the Bureau of Indian Affairs and reservation schools, and other federal agencies serving Indian peoples under the "trust responsibility." Fighting legal battles to protect tribal rights and develop resources proved costly, however, and governments looked to new sources of revenue. Some of these sources were controversial.

THE PEOPLE AND THE LAND IN CONFLICT

Under its longtime chair Wendell Chino, the Mescalero Apache Tribal Council aggressively sought ways to enhance the tribe's economic position. Like tribes elsewhere, the Mescalero established gaming operations, that is, legalized gambling, at its Inn of the Mountain Gods resort facility. This position pitted it against the state of New Mexico, which sought to regulate and control tribal gaming operations. The Mescalero and other tribes fought back, insisting on their right to administer reservations without state interference. More controversial within the tribe and the state, however, was the tribal government's decision to allow the reservation to become a temporary repository for spent nuclear fuel.

Both the U.S. Department of Energy and the nuclear energy industry faced the predicament of finding a permanent, safe, and stable geologic storage site for spent nuclear fuel rods. Eastern states, where most of the nuclear power plants were found, refused to store the spent rods. Lawmakers and industry leaders, then, looked to the West with its smaller population and open spaces. Consensus seemed to be developing around Yucca Mountain in Nevada as a permanent site, but preparing it was still decades away. In the meantime, temporary sites would have to be found.

Chino and members of the council believed that a 450-acre (182-hectare) site on the western slope of Sierra Blanca, the 12,000-foot (3,650-meter) peak that dominated the reservation, would be ideal. Thirty thousand metric tons (33,069 tons) of waste could be stored in concrete bunkers, earning the tribe up to $25 million a year over the facility's 40-year life span. To reporters following the story, Fred Peso, vice chair, also pointed out that the tribe, relatively young, was facing a population boom and tribal median income was still only half of New Mexico's. Future Mescalero needed the hundreds of good-paying jobs the new industry would provide.

Yet against this vision of tribal prosperity, critics of the Mescalero plan, environmental organizations, and the state of New Mexico held up the Chernobyl disaster of 1986, which saw a cloud of radioactive fallout jeopardize the health and well-being of thousands in the Soviet Union while degrading the environment. In an article in the *Natural Resources Journal*, Chino lashed out. "Do [you] believe that we Indians are so poor and pathetic, our leadership so greedy and dictatorial, as to risk the health and safety of our people? Do you believe we would deliberately contaminate what little remains of our ancestral homelands? . . . Of course not." "Paternalism is alive and well," he added, "decades after the white man took over our ancestral lands. We got a little piece of land that is still in jeopardy of being chipped away by threats to our sovereignty. The Mescalero Apache are a proud and accomplished tribe—and until people have taken an impartial view from the walk in our moccasins—it would seem we will never have the equality reserved for other U.S. citizens."

Some Mescalero, however, expressed doubts about the council's plans. They too pointed to possible environmental damage to the land as well as to people's long-term health. Among these, Rufina Marie Laws, newly returned to the reservation, led the fight. In an interview with reporter Ken Verdoia, she explained that a vision had inspired her to take up the cause:

> When I realized the meaning of the vision and understood the path that I had to take, I did not go into this path willingly. I realized that I had a choice. I could remain silent and be a follower of a dangerous plan or I could remember the seventh

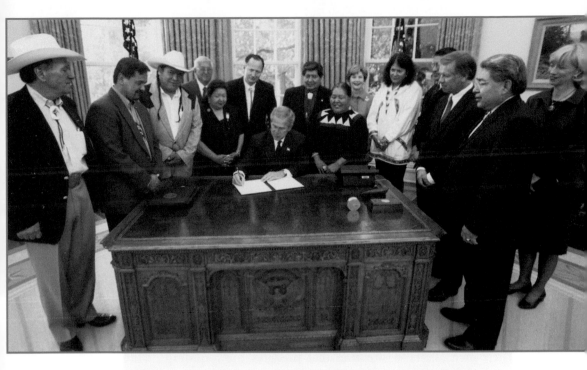

With Native American leaders from all over the United States looking on, President George W. Bush signs a Memorandum on Tribal Sovereignty and Consultation. This document renews the federal government's commitment to working with Native American reservations on a government-to-government basis.

generation. The seventh generation means that one's decisions in life . . . great or small, positive or negative . . . impacts others and many times reaches as far as the seventh generation. . . . When the time comes and a child from the seventh generation asks that individual, "What did you do when that decision was made on earth? Asked to go into nuclear waste as a business enterprise, where did you stand? What decision did you make at that time?" . . . The vision I had showed me facing such a child, and explaining why I was responsible for the horror they faced because of nuclear waste on our tribal lands.

On January 31, 1995, in a referendum, members of the tribe voted 490 to 362 against the proposal. The council, though, launched a petition drive for a revote, a procedure allowed under the tribal constitution. This time supporters of the nuclear waste facility won, 593 to 372. But the victory was short-lived. In April 1996, negotiations between the tribe and power plant officials broke down, and the storage facility was never constructed. By 1998 Chino himself was dead, struck by a fatal heart attack.

As the dispute at Mescalero demonstrates, Apache disagreed on different approaches to development and used the political process to express those differences. Such political expression is a function of self-government. For the Apache and all other American Indian tribes, self-government is a function of their sovereignty.

APACHE SOVEREIGNTY

Tribal sovereignty grows out of the history of tribes managing their own affairs, a situation that predates the founding of the United States. When the United States organized itself as a sovereign nation, its Constitution recognized the special status of tribes and recognized their sovereignty. This is why treaties, agreements between sovereign nations, were so often used to formalize relations. As the United States expanded, it encompassed more and more territory, in the process opening relations with more and more tribes. From the perspective of the federal government, these tribes are "nations within a nation," self-governing bodies within the boundaries of the United States, ultimately subject to the Constitution and federal authority, expressed through the Congress. When the Fort Sill Apache Tribe organized a federally recognized tribal government in the 1970s, for example, it joined the other 560 federally recognized American Indian tribes in the United States that are self-governing as a factor of their sovereignty.

Tribal sovereignty is not absolute, however. The jurisdiction of the tribal government is not always clear, especially in matters that might affect another self-governing entity, such as a state.

When the Mescalero Apache Tribal Council considered storing nuclear waste material on reservation land in the 1990s, the state of New Mexico was vitally interested, as it knew that potential environmental damage would not respect tribal boundaries but would spill over, potentially affecting the health and welfare of thousands of people. As a result, it argued that it should have some say over the tribal decision and looked to the federal government to support its stance.

In such cases, states and tribes have to trust that the United States government will always act in their best interests. With tribes, this "trust responsibility" of the United States is even more important, as often treaties resulted in tribes giving up certain rights to the United States in exchange for promises specifically dealing with tribal welfare. Sometimes these promises have interfered with tribal sovereignty, particularly when the federal government itself has taken on the management of tribal or individual assets. In general, however, tribes, like the 50 states that make up the union, often look to the federal government for the additional resources necessary to provide for their people's general health, education, and well-being. Yet unlike the states, they have often had to forcefully remind the federal government of its responsibilities.

FEDERALLY RECOGNIZED APACHE TRIBES

The United States now recognizes nine separate Apache tribes, either through a previous treaty relationship, action taken by the Department of the Interior, or an act of Congress. Given the long history of interaction between the American government and different Apache groups—interaction that included warfare, forced relocation, and imprisonment—it is not surprising that not all federally recognized Apache tribes correspond perfectly to historic bands. The Fort Sill Apache Tribe, for example, is made up of the descendants of different Chiricahua groups that lived in Arizona and New Mexico. Other Chiricahua make up part of the federally

Cultural Sovereignty

Sovereignty involves much more than governing reservations and regulating tribal affairs. Sovereignty also concerns ownership and control of cultural resources. Many American Indian tribes have been engaged in long-running battles to reassert control over sacred places and sacred objects, including human remains. In 1990 federal legislation finally resulted from these efforts. The Native American Graves Protection and Repatriation Act, commonly referred to as NAGPRA, requires all institutions receiving federal funds to inventory their collections of Native American artifacts and human remains and share these lists with American Indian tribes. Tribes may then request the repatriation or return of these items.

In response to this legislation, the Apache tribes of Arizona formed the Western Apache NAGPRA Working Group, a joint enterprise of the San Carlos, White Mountain, and Tonto Apache Tribes and the Apache of the Yavapai-Apache Nation.

recognized Mescalero Apache Tribe, as do a number of Lipan Apache. In other cases, some recognized tribes are made up of two distinct groups sharing one reservation (although some merging could and did occur over time). The Yavapai-Apache Tribe, for instance, contains both Yavapai and Tonto Apache people (a band among the Western Apache) who were brought together when many Apache and other Indian peoples were concentrated at San Carlos Reservation in the nineteenth century. Later relocated to a new reservation northwest of San Carlos, the Yavapai and Tonto Apache were then formally recognized as one tribe under the Indian Reorganization Act process.

Like the states, tribes come in different shapes and sizes. Some are quite small, such as the Tonto Apache Tribe, which received federal recognition in 1972. With a little more than 140 members, the

By 2009 their efforts had resulted in the repatriation of 38 sacred or culturally significant objects from the Smithsonian Institution in Washington and an additional 302 objects from 20 other institutions.

Many of the objects repatriated are considered living beings, manifestations of the spiritual force—the power— that the Apache say permeates the universe. Accordingly, the packing crates that held the Smithsonian objects were pierced with breathing holes. A medicine man used sacred pollen to bless the shipment as well. In Arizona, Apache elders returned the artifacts to the mountains and other scared sites known only to the people.

The return of sacred objects is directly connected to the social and spiritual health of the Apache people. As Vincent Randall, a Yavapai-Apache, explained to Kenneth Fletcher writing for Smithsonian.com, "The elders told us that they need to come home out of respect. Otherwise the consequences of fooling around with these things are alcoholism, suicide, domestic violence, and all of society's woes."

tribal land base is only 85 acres (34 ha), located adjacent to the town of Payson, Arizona. The Yavapai-Apache Tribe of the Camp Verde Reservation in Arizona is also small, made up of about 1,000 people with a land base of some 640 acres (259 ha). Another small group in Arizona is found on the Fort McDowell Mohave-Apache Reservation, containing Yavapai, Mohave, and Apache Indian peoples. The White Mountain Apache Tribe of the Fort Apache Reservation, on the other hand, number over 10,000 with a land base of more than 1.6 million acres (647,497 ha). The largest Apache reservation in Arizona, the San Carlos Reservation, home to the San Carlos Apache Tribe, is more than 1.8 million acres (728,434 ha) in size. The 10,000 people living there are descended from many Apache bands.

Other federally recognized Apache tribes are found in New Mexico. The Jicarilla Apache Tribe numbers over 3,000

Although the federal government does not recognize all Apache tribes, more than 57,000 people have identified themselves as Apache. Many are maintaining Apache culture and traditions and teach their children about their heritage.

individuals, two-thirds of whom still live on the reservation of more than 870,000 acres (352,076 ha). The Mescalero Apache Reservation, located in the southeastern part of New Mexico, is home to the Mescalero Apache Tribe. More than 3,600 people live on the 460,000-acre (186,155-ha) reservation. Finally, other federally recognized tribes are found in Oklahoma, most quite small. The Apache Tribe of Oklahoma, descendants of the people known as the Kiowa-Apache, has more than 1,300 enrolled members with a tribal land base of almost 282,000 acres (114,121 ha). The Fort Sill Apache Tribe has nearly 350 enrolled members.

Like Americans everywhere, the pursuit of economic opportunity has taken many Apache people to different communities and states. Military service plays a role in this migration as well. Yet, many still retain strong ties to their homelands and particularly their relatives. Enrolled tribal members, however, capture but a portion of the Apache population in the United States. Some individuals who are ethnically Apache may not hold official membership in a federally recognized tribe (another attribute of sovereignty is the ability to define tribal membership requirements) or may be members of unrecognized tribes, such as the Lipan Apache Tribe of Texas, organized as a nonprofit corporation. These people, however, readily identify with their Apache ancestry. Probably this is most clearly expressed in federal census data that is based on an individual's self-identification. The 2000 census, for example, counted 57,199 people who identified themselves as solely Apache (some officially enrolled tribal members and some not). The same census, however, for the first time allowed respondents to identify themselves as belonging to more than one racial or ethnic category. Based on this data, Apache numbers climbed to 104,556.

The 100,000 or so people who call themselves Apache make up only a small piece of the fabric of American society. Yet, beyond Apache numbers lie deeper meanings. Apache culture has persisted for millennia, not inert and unchanging, but creative and adaptable. Over their history, the people have moved from tundra and mountains and plains to towns and cities. They have come across Pueblos, Spaniards, Mexicans, Europeans, and Anglo-Americans. These encounters continue today, each creating new stories that overlay the old, providing lessons and guidance for future generations.

Chronology

ʏʏʏʏʏʏʏʏʏʏ

Circa 1500   Apache groups appear on the fringes of the Southwest.

1540s   The Coronado expedition encounters Querechos on the Texas plains, one of the first accounts of Spanish contact with the Apache.

1600s   The Apache diverge into western and eastern orientation groups. Peaceful trade contacts at Pueblo villages and raiding are both in evidence.

Timeline

Circa 1500

Apache groups appear on the fringes of the Southwest

1835 and 1837

Apache and Comanche raids into Mexico intensify

1848

The Treaty of Guadalupe Hidalgo results in the transfer of much of the Apache homelands to the jurisdiction of the United States

1600

1835

1600s

Apache diverge into western and eastern orientation groups

1793

Eight peace establishments harbor more than 2,000 Apache people

1760s–1770s	Apache raids reach serious proportions. Spanish policy-makers begin administrative reforms in response.
1786	The Gálvez Policy, introduced to "pacify" the Apache, is the basis for the formation of peace establishments.
1793	Eight peace establishments harbor more than 2,000 Apache. Raiding diminishes to manageable proportions in northern New Spain.
1821	Mexican independence. Mexican states are unable to maintain the peace establishment program.
1835 and 1837	Apache and Comanche raids into Mexico intensify. The Mexican states of Chihuahua and Sonora institute "scalp" laws, paying a bounty for Apache scalps in a war of extermination.

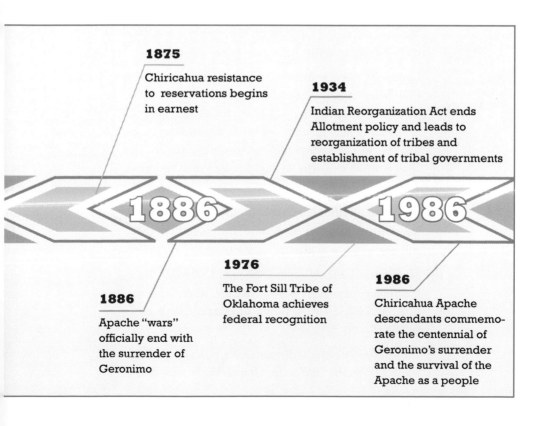

1875
Chiricahua resistance to reservations begins in earnest

1934
Indian Reorganization Act ends Allotment policy and leads to reorganization of tribes and establishment of tribal governments

1886   1986

1976
The Fort Sill Tribe of Oklahoma achieves federal recognition

1886
Apache "wars" officially end with the surrender of Geronimo

1986
Chiricahua Apache descendants commemorate the centennial of Geronimo's surrender and the survival of the Apache as a people

1846	Mexico and the United States go to war. Mangas Coloradas of the Chiricahua Apache pledges friendship to the Americans.
1848	The Treaty of Guadalupe Hidalgo, ending the Mexican-American War, results in the transfer of much of the Apache homelands to the jurisdiction of the United States. The United States promises to end Apache raids into Mexico.
1853	The Treaty of Fort Atkinson is signed with Comanche, Kiowa, and Kiowa-Apache, allowing the United States to build roads across the plains. The United States also promises to provide annuities. Both sides pledge peace and an end to raiding.
1854	The United States acquires more of the Apache homelands with the Gadsden Purchase treaty with Mexico. The United States also ends responsibility for Apache raids into Mexico from American soil.
1858	Mexican forces kill Geronimo's wife, mother, and children. Geronimo swears revenge against the Mexicans.
1861	Lieutenant George Bascom treacherously captures the Chiricahua Apache leader Cochise, accusing him of raiding and kidnapping. Cochise escapes, but Bascom continues to hold members of his family and band captive. Eventually, six Apache warriors are executed. The "Bascom Affair" ignites conflict between the Chiricahua and the U.S. Army.
1862	Mescalero Apache are relocated to the Bosque Redondo; they are later joined by the Navajo. Eventually both tribes will be allowed to return to their homelands.
1863	Miners treacherously capture Mangas Coloradas. He is turned over to soldiers at Fort McLane, where he is tortured and killed "while trying to escape." His body is mutilated.
1871	Disgruntled Arizona settlers attack a peaceful encampment of Apache at Camp Grant. The Camp Grant

Massacre contributes to changes in government Indian policy.

General George Crook assumes command of the Department of Arizona. All Apache are ordered onto reservations. Military operations are opened against those Apache who resist.

Crook begins to enroll companies of Apache scouts.

1872	General O.O. Howard and Cochise agree to the formation of the Chiricahua Reservation. The San Carlos and Fort Apache reservations are established by executive order.
1874	Cochise dies. John Clum is appointed agent for the San Carlos Reservation.
1875	The U.S. government begins to concentrate most of the Western Apache on the San Carlos Reservation. Chiricahua resistance to concentration and reservations begins in earnest.
1886	Apache "wars" officially end with the surrender of Geronimo. Chiricahua Apache are made prisoners of war.
1887	A reservation for Jicarilla Apache in northern New Mexico is created by executive order.
	Congress passes the General Allotment Act to begin the process of dissolving reservations and assigning land to individual Indians. Eventually the Oklahoma Apache, including Fort Sill and Kiowa-Apache, undergo Allotment, as do the Jicarilla Apache in New Mexico.
1894	Chiricahua Apache prisoners are relocated to Fort Sill, Oklahoma.
1913	Chiricahua Apache are released. Most move to the Mescalero Apache Reservation in New Mexico. Some remain in Oklahoma.

1921	Silas John Edwards begins the "Holy Grounds" movement at the Fort Apache Reservation, urging Apache people to reform their lives.
1924	The Indian Citizenship Act extends citizenship and voting rights to all American Indians.
1928	*The Problem of Indian Administration*, the so-called Meriam Report, is published. It makes policy recommendations to deal with problems of poverty and ill health found on reservations and criticizes educational practices. Apache are among those interviewed for the report, which gives impetus to the Indian Reorganization Act.
	Alchesay of the White Mountain Apache dies. He helped to maintain traditional leadership among the tribe during the reservation years.
1934	The Indian Reorganization Act ends Allotment policy and leads to the reorganization of tribes and the establishment of tribal governments. Western Apache tribes, Mescalero Apache, and Jicarilla Apache organize tribal governments.
1941	The United States enters World War II. Apache in large numbers enlist and fight overseas.
1946	The Indian Claims Commission Act establishes the Indian Claims Court. A number of Apache tribes eventually receive settlements from the court to compensate for lost lands.
1953	Termination policy is introduced with the intent of ending the trust relationship between the United States and American Indian tribes. Fort Sill Apache are targeted for Termination.
	Relocation policy is introduced to encourage American Indians to move to urban areas and enter into "mainstream" America. Some Mescalero Apache relocate to Los Angeles but soon return.
1954	The White Mountain Apache Tribal Council creates the White Mountain Recreation Enterprise to increase tribal

income through the development and promotion of fishing, hunting, camping, and other tourist activities. Other Apache tribes form similar enterprises in the 1950s and 1960s to develop tribal resources.

1975 The Indian Self-Determination and Education Assistance Act sees tribes exert more authority over federal assistance programs.

1976 The Fort Sill Apache Tribe of Oklahoma achieves federal recognition. Mildred Imoch Cleghorn becomes its first tribal chair.

1986 Chiricahua Apache descendants commemorate the centennial of Geronimo's surrender and the survival of the Apache as a people.

1990 Congress passes the Native American Graves Protection and Repatriation Act, commonly referred to as NAGPRA. NAGPRA requires all institutions receiving federal funds to inventory their collections of Native American artifacts and human remains and share these lists with Native American tribes. Tribes may then request the repatriation or return of these items. Apache tribes are active in seeking the return of sacred objects.

1998 Wendell Chino, longtime chair of the Mescalero Apache Tribe, dies. During his time in office, he helped raise the tribe from poverty to prosperity. His last years in office were controversial when he pushed for the establishment of a nuclear waste repository on the Mescalero Reservation.

2009 The House of Representatives passes House Resolution 132, honoring the life and memory of Chiricahua Apache leader Geronimo, in an effort to bring "healing" to the Apache and American relationship.

Glossary

agent A person appointed by the Bureau of Indian Affairs to supervise U.S. government programs on a reservation and/or in a specific region.

anthropology The branch of the social sciences concerned with the study of humanity. The field also has elements of the humanities and the natural sciences.

archaeology The study of the human past, primarily through material evidence such as artifacts (like bones, tools, housing, clothing, and shelter) and the environmental record.

Bureau of Indian Affairs The U.S. government agency charged with handling matters related to Indians in the United States.

ethnography A branch of anthropology that deals with the scientific description of individual human societies.

General Allotment Act Enacted in 1887, the act provided for the division of tribally held lands into individually owned parcels and the opening up of "surplus" lands to resettlement by non-Indians.

Great Society The popular name of the progressive social welfare and civil rights legislation of the Lyndon Johnson administration (1963–1969).

Indian Reorganization Act (IRA) The 1934 federal law that ended the policy of allotting plots of land to individuals and encouraged the development of reservation communities. The act also provided for the creation of autonomous tribal governments.

matrilineal Relating to descent or kinship through the female line.

matrilocal Relating to residence with the wife's family or tribe.

Meriam Report A U.S. government study in 1928 that found appalling conditions of poverty on many reservations and suggested increased federal funding to Native American tribes.

mescal Either of two species of spineless, dome-shaped cactus (also called *peyote*); an intoxicating beverage distilled from the fermented juice of certain species of agave.

Native American Graves Protection and Repatriation Act of 1990 A law that allows Native American tribes to repossess the artifacts and grave remains that were taken from them by museums and individual collectors.

peace establishments Places where the Apache were encouraged to settle, receive rations, take up farming, learn Spanish ways, and eventually become productive citizens of northern New Spain. Peace establishments were introduced in the late 1700s and lasted into the early 1800s.

repatriation The process of returning an object to its original owners.

reservation A tract of land retained by Indians for their own occupation and use.

sovereignty A nation or state's supreme power within its borders.

wickiup A dome-shaped dwelling place covered in hides.

Bibliography

Ball, Eve, and James Kaywaykla. *In the Days of Victorio: Recollections of a Warm Springs Apache*. Tucson: University of Arizona Press, 1970.

Basso, Keith H., ed. *Western Apache Raiding and Warfare: From the Notes of Grenville Goodwin*. Tucson: University of Arizona Press, 1971.

Basso, Keith H. *Western Apache Language and Culture: Essays in Linguistic Anthropology*. Tucson: University of Arizona Press, 1990.

———. *Wisdom Sits in Places: Landscape and Language Among the Western Apache*. Albuquerque: University of New Mexico Press, 1996.

Betzinez, Jason, with William Sturtevant Nye. *I Fought with Geronimo*. Lincoln: University of Nebraska Press, 1987.

Bittle, William E. "A Brief History of the Kiowa Apache." *University of Oklahoma Papers in Anthropology* 12, no. 1 (1971): 1–34.

Boyer, Ruth McDonald, and Narcissus Duffy Gayton. *Apache Mothers and Daughters: Four Generations of a Family*. Norman and London: University of Oklahoma Press, 1992.

Buchanan, Kimberly Moore. "Apache Women Warriors." *Southwestern Studies Series* 79, El Paso: Texas Western Press, 1986.

Chebahtah, William, and Nancy McGown Minor. *Chevato: The Story of the Apache Warrior Who Captured Herman Lehmann*. Lincoln and London: University of Nebraska Press, 2007.

Chino, Wendell. "Response to 'The Mescalero Apache Indians and Monitored Retrievable Storage of Spent Nuclear Fuel: A Study in Environmental Ethics.'" *Natural Resources Journal* 36, no. 4 (1996): 913–919.

Colomeda, Lorelei Anne Lambert. *Keepers of the Central Fire: Issues in Ecology for Indigenous Peoples*. Sudbury, Mass.: Jones and Bartlett Publishers, 1999.

Coppersmith, Clifford Patrick. "Cultural Survival and a Native American Community: The Chiricahua and Warm Springs Apache in Oklahoma, 1913–1996." Ph.D. Dissertation, Oklahoma State University, 1996.

Cornell, Stephen, and Marta C. Gil-Swedberg. "Sociohistorical Factors in American Indian Economic Development: A Comparison of

Three Apache Cases." *Harvard Project on American Indian Economic Development*, 1992.

Cremony, John C. *Life Among the Apache*. Lincoln and London: University of Nebraska Press, 1983.

Delay, Brian. "Independent Indians and the U.S.-Mexican War." *American Historical Review* 112 (2007): 35–68.

Dobyns, Henry F. *The Apache People*. Phoenix, Ariz.: Indian Tribal Series, 1971.

———. *The Mescalero Apache People*. Phoenix, Ariz.: Indian Tribal Series, 1973.

Fletcher, Kenneth R. "The Road to Repatriation." Smithsonian.com, November 25, 2008. Available online. URL: http://www.smith sonianmag.com/specialsections/heritage/the-road-to-repatriation. html.

Franco, Jeré Bishop. *Crossing the Pond: The Native American Effort in World War II*. Denton: University of North Texas Press, 1999.

Froebel, Julius. *Seven Years Travel in Central America, Northern Mexico, and the Far West of the United States*. London: Richard Bentley, 1859.

Gálvez, Bernardo de. *Instructions for Governing the Interior Provinces of New Spain, 1786*. Translated and edited by Donald E. Worcester. Berkeley, Calif.: Quivira Society, 1951.

Geronimo. *Geronimo: His Own Story*, as told to S.M. Barrett. New York: Penguin Books, 1996.

Goodwin, Grenville, and Charles Kaut. "A Native Religious Movement Among the White Mountain and Cibecue Apache." *Southwestern Journal of Anthropology* 10 (1954): 385–404.

Griffen, William B. "The Compás: A Chiricahua Apache Family of the Late 18th and Early 19th Centuries." *American Indian Quarterly* 7 (Spring 1983): 21–49.

Griffin-Pierce, Trudy. *Chiricahua Apache Enduring Power: Naiche's Puberty Ceremony Paintings*. Tuscaloosa: University of Alabama Press, 2006.

Hämäläinen, Pekka. "The Rise and Fall of the Plains Indian Horse Cultures." *Journal of American History* 90, (2003): 833–862.

Iverson, Peter. *When Indians Became Cowboys: Native Peoples and Cattle Ranching in the American West*. Norman: University of Oklahoma Press, 1994.

Johnson, George. "Dispute over Indian Casinos in New Mexico Produces Quandary on Law and Politics." *New York Times*, August 18, 1996.

KUED-TV. "Rufina Marie Laws, Anti-Nuclear Activist, Mescalero Apache Reservation." Interview by Ken Verdoia. 2001. Available online. URL: http://www.kued.org/productions/skullvalley/documentary/interviews/laws.html.

Lamar, Howard Roberts. *The Far Southwest, 1846–1912: A Territorial History*. New York: W. W. Norton and Company, 1970.

Loendorf, Lawrence L. *Thunder and Herds: Rock Art of the High Plains*. Walnut Creek, Calif.: Left Coast Press, 2008.

Meriam, Lewis, et. al. *The Problem of Indian Administration*. Baltimore, Md.: Johns Hopkins Press, 1928.

Opler, Morris E. *An Apache Lifeway: The Economic, Social, and Religious Institutions of the Chiricahua Indians*. Chicago: The University of Chicago Press, 1941.

———. *Myths and Tales of the Chiricahua Apache Indians*. Lincoln and London: University of Nebraska Press, 1994.

———. *Apache Odyssey: A Journey between Two Worlds*. Lincoln and London: University of Nebraska Press, 2002.

Osburn, Katherine Marie Birmingham. "The Navajo at the Bosque Redondo: Cooperation Resistance, and Initiative, 1864–1868." *New Mexico Historical Review* 60, no. 4: 399–413.

Perry, Richard J. *Western Apache Heritage: People of the Mountain Corridor*. Austin: University of Texas Press, 1991.

———. *Apache Reservation: Indigenous Peoples and the American State*. Austin: University of Texas Press, 1993.

Robinson, Sherry. *Apache Voices: Their Stories of Survival as Told to Eve Ball*. Albuquerque: University of New Mexico Press, 2000.

Rushing III, W. Jackson. *Allan Houser: An American Master (Chiricahua Apache, 1914–1994)*. New York: Harry N. Abrams, 2004.

Sachs, Noah. "The Mescalero Apache Indians and Monitored Retrievable Storage of Spent Nuclear Fuel: A Study in Environmental Ethics." *Natural Resources Journal* 36, no. 4 (1996): 881–912.

Sonnichsen, C.L. *The Mescalero Apaches*. Norman: University of Oklahoma Press, 1958.

Spicer, Edward H. *Cycles of Conquest: The Impact of Spain, Mexico, and the United States on the Indians of the Southwest, 1533–1960*. Tucson and London: University of Arizona Press, 1992.

Stockel, H. Henrietta. *Women of the Apache Nation: Voices of Truth*. Reno: University of Nevada Press, 1991.

Sweeney, Edwin R. *Mangas Coloradas: Chief of the Chiricahua Apache.* Norman: University of Oklahoma Press, 1998.

Thrapp, Dan L. *The Conquest of Apacheria.* Norman: University of Oklahoma Press, 1967.

West, Elliott. *The Contested Plains: Indians, Goldseekers, and the Rush to Colorado.* Lawrence: University Press of Kansas, 1998.

Whitewolf, Jim. *The Life of a Kiowa Apache Indian.* Edited by Charles S. Brant. New York: Dover Publications, 1969.

Further Resources

Books

Aleshire, Peter. *Cochise: The Life and Times of the Great Apache Chief*. Edison, N.J.: Castle Books, 2005.

Boyer, Ruth McDonald, and Narcissus Duffy Gayton. *Apache Mothers and Daughters: Four Generations of a Family*. Norman and London: University of Oklahoma Press, 1997.

Geronimo. *Geronimo: His Own Story*, as told to S.M. Barrett. New York: Penguin Books, 1996.

Opler, Morris E. *Myths and Tales of the Chiricahua Apache Indians*. Lincoln and London: University of Nebraska Press, 1994.

Roberts, David. *Once They Moved Like the Wind: Cochise, Geronimo, and the Apache Wars*. New York: Touchstone, 1994.

Robinson, Sherry. *Apache Voices: Their Stories of Survival as Told to Eve Ball*, Albuquerque: University of New Mexico Press, 2003.

Shapard, Bud. *Chief Loco: Apache Peacemaker*. Norman: University of Oklahoma Press, 2010.

Sweeney, Edwin R. *Cochise: Chiricahua Apache Chief*. Norman: University of Oklahoma Press, 1991.

———. *Mangas Coloradas: Chief of the Chiricahua Apaches*. Norman: University of Oklahoma Press, 1998.

Web Sites

Countries and Their Cultures: Apaches
http://www.everyculture.com/multi/A-Br/Apaches.html
The "Apaches" section of the Countries and Their Cultures Web site provides a wealth of information concerning Apache history and culture, including dances, songs, holidays, literature, and the arts.

Inter-Tribal Council of Arizona
http://www.itcaonline.com

All of the Arizona Apache Tribes are members of the Inter-Tribal Council of Arizona. The site gives links to each tribe, describing their locations, current government and council members, and special attractions/events for visitors.

Mescalero Apache Tribe
http://www.mescaleroapache.com
This tribal Web site provides extensive information about reservation attractions, tribal economic enterprises, culture and history, government, and other topics.

U.S. Census Bureau
http://www.census.gov
The U.S. Census Bureau provides extensive information on American Indian people, including the Apache. Population, housing, income, and median income are only some of the areas on which the bureau collects data.

Films

Geronimo and the Apache Resistance. Produced by Neil Goodwin and Lena Carr. 1988. Alexandria, Va.: PBS Video.

Picture Credits

Index

About the Contributors

⅄⅄⅄⅄⅄⅄⅄⅄⅄⅄⅄⅄⅄⅄⅄

JOSEPH C. JASTRZEMBSKI is professor of history and coordinator of the Native American Studies Program at Minot State University in North Dakota. He specializes in nineteenth-century Native American history. His research interests include the cultures of the Southwest and Plains, ethnohistory, folklore, and museum studies. Jastrzembski is also codirector of the Mandan Language and Oral Traditions Preservation Project.

Series editor **PAUL C. ROSIER** received his Ph.D. in American History from the University of Rochester in 1998. Dr. Rosier currently serves as Associate Professor of History at Villanova University (Villanova, Pennsylvania), where he teaches Native American History, American Environmental History, Global Environmental Justice Movements, History of American Capitalism, and World History.

In 2001, the University of Nebraska Press published his first book, *Rebirth of the Blackfeet Nation, 1912–1954*; in 2003, Greenwood Press published *Native American Issues* as part of its Contemporary Ethnic American Issues series. In 2006, he coedited an international volume called *Echoes from the Poisoned Well: Global Memories of Environmental Injustice*. Dr. Rosier has also published articles in the *American Indian Culture and Research Journal*, the *Journal of American Ethnic History*, and *The Journal of American History*. His *Journal of American History* article, entitled "They Are Ancestral Homelands: Race, Place, and Politics in Cold War Native America, 1945–1961," was selected for inclusion in *The Ten Best History Essays of 2006–2007*, published by Palgrave MacMillan in 2008; and it won the Western History Association's 2007 Arrell Gibson Award for Best Essay on the history of Native Americans. His latest book, *Serving Their Country: American Indian Politics and Patriotism in the Twentieth Century* (Harvard University Press), is winner of the 2010 Labriola Center American Indian National Book Award